DAVID P. CAMPBELL

ASSOCIATE PROFESSOR OF PSYCHOLOGY
UNIVERSITY OF MINNESOTA

THE RESULTS OF COUNSELING:
Twenty-Five Years Later

W. B. SAUNDERS COMPANY
Philadelphia and London

The Results of Counseling

To My Mother

FOREWORD

In prosecuting the research reported in the following pages, Dr. Campbell ingeniously has taken advantage of my "pack rat" way of life, learned from D. G. Paterson, of not discarding *any* data. Unknown to and uninspired by me, he discovered stored data of an earlier study of mine, made with W.P.A. funds in the depression years, published with Dr. Edward Bordin as co-author. As far as I know, Dr. Campbell's longitudinal study is the only one of its kind; and I hope it will inspire other researchers to study the result of counseling over long time spans.

Moreover, I hope that in line with the early Birmingham experiments, Dr. Campbell's definitive inquiry as to any long-term residuals of short-term counseling (1 to 3 interviews) will add impetus to the further delineation of the selective factors related to seeking the counseling relationship. "What kinds of students seek counseling?" has long been a most perplexing unknown variable in this category of research. Now we have some preliminary indication that counseling "readiness" may be characterized as a mild (?) anxiousness, as well as an openness to consider new and relevant data about oneself as potential and newly perceived options for one's choice of life goals. Replication of this study is, of course, indicated in the hardheaded Minnesota tradition of critical inquiry.

In interpreting the delineated (small) differences between counseled and (matched) non-counseled individuals, we must speculate about the possible influences of the *Zeitgeist*, the depressing Depression decade during which anxiety as to the possibility of discovering a life occupation was indeed a vector force in the lives of college-age adolescents. Probably research will reveal that similar anxiety as to the future is characteristic of all adolescents during all time spans.

It would have been gratifying to D. G. Paterson to read this report. It was he who pioneered with others in adapting the industrial selection and placement methods of Munsterberg (imported from European industrial psychology), along with those forged in the World War I placement of army recruits, to the selection, placement and counseling of college students. Our present national policies of manpower utilization would be less effective had it not been for these pioneerings in applied psychology. Although we currently profit from incorporating new insights and new knowledge about human potentiality from personality theory and therapy, still the hardheaded experimental design of those pioneers forged techniques and instruments that are still relevant to today's counseling of adolescents.

I am confident that in decades ahead Dr. Campbell's pioneering in this study and in his restructuring of methods of measuring "interests" will prove to be as seminal as are the innovations of the earlier applied psychologists.

I am most pleased to have been instrumental in storing data for his study, just as his graduate students of future years will be grateful for his newly established data bank of completed interest inventories, drawn both from Strong's work at Stanford and our files at Minnesota. Not only has he inherited E. K. Strong's massive archives of interest data, he is one of "E. K.'s" professional successors in research.

E. G. WILLIAMSON

PREFACE

My office at the University of Minnesota is in Eddy Hall, one of the oldest buildings on campus. From the outside, the distinguishing characteristics are the adornments of its age, such as the turret and the wind vane. Inside, up under the slanting ceilings of the top floors, are packed the University's student information files. They are very extensive as, under policies instigated by D. G. Paterson and E. G. Williamson, hardly anything has been thrown away at Minnesota in the last 45 years.

One of the pay-offs of these policies is the research reported in the following pages. With the use of the old files, it has been possible to trace the development of a sample of students over a considerable length of time. This type of longitudinal study would not be possible in most other institutions.

Although it was the presence of these old data that really made this project possible, several other acknowledgments need to be made. The University's Student Counseling Bureau, under the direction of Ralph F. Berdie, provided the space and allowed me virtually unlimited freedom to pursue these goals. The financing came, for the most part, from the Cooperative Research Branch of the U. S. Office of Education under projects 1346 and 2160. Permission to use materials published elsewhere has been given by the editor of the *Journal of Counseling Psychology*, the McGraw-Hill Publishing Company, and the Educational Testing Service.

Several other people have had a hand in this project. Ted Volsky originally was one of the principal investigators and was involved in the planning stages before he left to become the Director of the Counseling Bureau at the University of Colorado. One of the real pleasures of this activity was the opportunity to work with a string of bright, capable, and industrious student research assistants, both graduate and undergraduate. Included in that group, at one time or another over the past four years, were Lee Becker, Suzanne DePree, Charlotte Fuller Kauppi, Charles Johansson, James Johnson, Judy Phillips, Jack Rossmann, Larry Swandby, Robert

Thorpe, Walter Warfield, and Lenore White Harmon. Some of these were more involved than others. Jack Rossmann's involvement is demonstrated by his co-authorship of the last chapter of this report; Charles Johansson is the only person besides myself who has been associated with this work from beginning to end. Starting on this project as a freshman, he gradually took over most of the responsibility for the data analysis.

Secretaries act as multipliers of one's productivity and I'm convinced that a good one can at least double one's output. In the seemingly endless rounds of correspondence, organizing files, and preparing manuscripts, I was fortunate to have two very good ones, Mrs. Barbara McHaffie and Mrs. Jean Forsberg.

The only person who really knows how deeply involved I have been in this project over the last four years is my wife, and the only ones who can appreciate her contribution are other women who have had both busy husbands and three little boys in four years.

The final word of grateful acknowledgment belongs to the participants in this research. Out of the blue one day they received a request for about five hours of their time, to include taking a college extrance examination—which threatened many of them considerably—and submitting to a prying, personal interview. Over 80 percent of them supplied all the information we asked for, usually willingly, and occasionally with gusto. Our interviewers were almost always well received, sometimes were wined and dined royally. Whatever merit this study has is due, in large part, to the cooperation of these individuals.

DAVID P. CAMPBELL
University of Minnesota

CONTENTS

ix

CHAPTER ONE

THE NEED FOR APPLIED RESEARCH IN THE HELPING PROFESSIONS

Counseling psychologists intend to help others. They share this goal with a variety of other professionals such as psychiatrists, social workers, ministers and YMCA secretaries. Like some of these, they also aspire to operate within a scientific framework in which causes and effects are known, in which processes are understood, and in which established truth is the guide rather than some abiding faith. However, most counseling practitioners would admit that, at the moment, in the counseling office faith is more abundant than truth. (And this is equally true of the other "helping professions.")

To a very large extent, faith (or, in another context, common sense) is a sufficient justification for much of what counseling psychologists do—the empirical establishment of some beneficial end is not necessary. For example, college counselors give information on courses and curricula. Proof, in the scientific sense, that this helps students is no more necessary than proof that the Information Window in the Administration Building is helpful.

As another example, students who are in considerable trouble find it helpful to talk with a sympathetic counselor. Even the most cynical professor, when confronted with a weeping co-ed, does not ask for the therapy success rate when he phones the counseling office for help.

While both of these examples illustrate the essential value—independent of scientific confirmation—of a counselor, they also illustrate that, if faith alone is the justification, it is not at all

1

apparent that what the counselor does could not be done just as well by a reasonably well-briefed, kindly grandmother.

If the counseling profession, or any other related profession, aspires to scientific status, it should establish systematically, for all to see, that it knows something of what it is doing. It had better know:

1. What kinds of people use its services.

2. What kinds of people join its ranks.

3. How to judge between a "good" and "bad" practitioner.

4. What is "good" and "bad" (that there is room for dissension here does not relieve the professional of the necessity of specifying his own criteria in publicly verifiable terms).

5. How to develop (or recognize) and use differential treatments.

6. The effects of such differential treatments.

7. How to recognize and measure, at least crudely, *relevant* differential qualities among those treated.

8. The relation between differential treatments and differential individual qualities.

This is not intended to be a systematic list; rather, it is a list of some of the things that a profession that intends to help others should be able to answer about itself.

To put the matter more specifically in counseling terms, the following is a list of beliefs, all of them held by various counselors, for which there is hardly a shred of scientific evidence:

> Counselors should not make decisions for their clients—the kids need to work things through for themselves.
> Students should not be shown their scores on interest inventories (or personality inventories) (or I.Q. tests).
> Counselors should be warm and accepting and not attempt to force their values on the counselees.
> Counseling should not be done by mail.
> The use of interest inventories in counseling helps the student to make wiser decisions.
> Students should be guided into curricula in which they will be happy and productive.
> Women counselors work better with women students.
> Counselors should never make the student angry.
> The counselor was a failure because the student didn't show up for a second interview.

The same sorts of statements could be generated for related professions, and the lack of an established foundation of fact would probably be equally embarrassing.

Raising the above questions in the first chapter would suggest that answers will be found in later pages, but they will not. Data are presented that bear on some of these questions; but after seeing the figures presented, any critical reader will surely have more unanswered questions than he had before. If that is not true, the book is decidedly a failure.

What I intend to do is talk about the generation of knowledge in one area, i.e., the long-term effects of counseling, and hope that this will stimulate both related work in counseling and similar long-range studies in other disciplines.

CHAPTER TWO

COUNSELED VERSUS NON-COUNSELED STUDENTS: CAN WE EXPECT DIFFERENCES?

To believe that one, two or even several hours of counseling received as a college freshman will create a distinguishable difference 25 years later in the adult requires either a large slice of foolish naïveté or a boundless optimism in the potential of the individual to change for the better. To actually put this belief of counseling impact to test probably requires more of the former than the latter. Nevertheless, this research has done that.

Two groups of students enrolled at the University of Minnesota 25 years ago (in the period of 1933 to 1940) were studied. Each contained about 400 students. One group had sought and received counseling as college freshmen; the other had not. An earlier study reported differences between these groups 25 years ago (Williamson and Bordin, 1940). Can we expect any detectable differences today? Most counseling psychologists would say "yes," or at least "I hope so," although they would probably be uneasy in their answer.

Common sense would dictate more pessimism. The influences, pressures, accidents, the good and bad breaks of life would almost certainly nullify any effect as fragile as a few hours with a counselor. In the particular group under study, college students of 25 years ago, these forces would be even more overwhelming.

Consider their history: They were teen-agers during the depression, college students in the immediate aftermath; they were thrown into World War II during their 20's and many had the youth and education most suited for front-line leadership. Almost all of the 350 men served in one capacity or another. At least one was killed in battle, another died in a POW camp, while a third fought a different kind of war for his ideals by choosing prison as a conscientious objector. The girls were WAC's or WAVE's, Link Trainer instructors, bandage rollers, or USO hostesses. A few became widows at an early age.

They have traveled like no other generation in history. Maybe the accommodations were not plush, but they saw the world. Shuttled from assignment to assignment, they had unusual opportunities to try out a variety of occupational experiences. Both during the war and after, they watched brand new occupations come into being. The number today in jobs that never existed during their college days is indicative: television writer, space scientist, computer programmer, manufacturer of teaching machines. No college student of 1935 wrote any of those job titles in the space on his admission blank asking for "occupational goal."

As adults, they both helped and were helped by the explosion of prosperity of the 1950's and today they are well off. Their median income is $14,500, and several of them net around $100,000 yearly. Over 70 percent of them make more than $10,000.

In the space of three decades they have seen bread lines and misery, have been shot at, either actually or vicariously, and now—on the average—live in $26,000 homes. Fully a sixth of them own not only a second car but a second home, usually in the form of a cabin, or perhaps a cabin cruiser.

After all of this, can we expect to find differences between counseled and non-counseled students today? Even if a difference was created by counseling, consider the technical difficulties of isolating it. Simply locating college students 25 years later is a formidable task, let alone assessing them in some manner. Does (and should) counseling make people more satisfied or more productive? How can either of these be measured? Was the control group of non-counseled students adequately comparable?

The groups might not differ even on the advice they received. The non-counseled students did not live in a vacuum. They undoubtedly sought advice and guidance from other faculty members, from their parents, from men in occupations they were considering entering, and from other students.

For all of these reasons, both historic and technical, any difference found between the groups would be surprising. Yet today they differ. Never very large, yet consistent enough to be meaningful, the differences reported in the following chapters show that *the counseled students today are mildly less satisfied with their station in life, but have more accomplishments to show for their efforts.* They report slightly less satisfaction with their jobs, their marriages, their social life, and their over-all situation. But they have won more degrees in college, more honors, and have more often been elected to leadership posts. Today they make a few dollars more each year (a statistically insignificant $1200) and score higher on a gross measure of "contribution to society."

The size of these differences is not dramatic, but that they exist at all is. Any other real differences are certainly obscured by the many methodological problems, the inadequate controls, the far from perfect measures, as well as the variety of counseling goals. Those differences that still appear rebut the earlier assertion of foolishness and naïveté among counseling adherents, and will probably add much to their optimism.

CHAPTER THREE

COUNSELING AT MINNESOTA 25 YEARS AGO

Any discussion of counseling effectiveness requires some comment on the type of counseling employed, the philosophy behind the counseling, and the specific techniques used.

Counseling at Minnesota, particularly that practiced in the Testing Bureau (now called the Student Counseling Bureau), has been dominated by one man, D. G. Paterson, and three of his students, E. G. Williamson, John G. Darley, and Ralph F. Berdie. Williamson was appointed as the first Director of the Testing Bureau in 1932. When he left in 1938 to become Dean of Students, Darley succeeded him as Director and served in that post until 1947. When Darley left to become Associate Dean of the Graduate School at Minnesota, Berdie took over the direction of the Student Counseling Bureau, and he holds that position today.

Over this 30-year period, the Student Counseling Bureau has evolved from a two or three man operation into a large service organization employing about 25 professional persons and a large supporting clerical staff. Its staff, mainly concerned with the counseling of the University students, has a wide range of other responsibilities, including administration of the Minnesota High School Statewide Testing Program, acting as consultants to the Admissions Office and the University's colleges and professional schools on matters of selection and placement, and providing a wide range of specialized services, such as counseling married students, working with disabled students, and providing technical advice on student personnel matters to the Minnesota high schools.

So much for the present; the intention in this chapter is to provide the reader with some of the flavor of the counseling practiced in the early 1930's at Minnesota to make the discussion in the following chapters more meaningful.

In his extensive history, *The University of Minnesota: 1851– 1951*, James Gray entitled one chapter, "Counseling: The Minnesota Point of View." In it he details the monumental amount of effort poured into student appraisal, advising, and guidance at the University, beginning just after World War I. Of the middle 1920's, he says (p. 353):

> Vocational counseling was expanded into a major function. While it aimed at a minimum of paternalism, the University's program called for as much practical help as possible in charting a student's course realistically.
>
> By 1928 the University had established as a stable technique the process of classifying all freshmen.* The next step in the development of a closely coordinated program was the creation in 1932 of the Testing Bureau. This was put under the direction of Edmund G. Williamson, who had joined the department of psychology six years before and who was in the process of earning his doctorate at Minnesota.
>
> Williamson was young (32), vigorous, and enthusiastic, and he needed to be, for in 1932 economic blight had reached the university and there was little money with which to develop the new educational units. But with a stubborn squaring of the jaw, this believer in the philosophy of responsibility spoke sharply to laissez-faire traditionalists:
>
> "The smug retort 'we cannot be expected to coddle our students' sounds suspiciously like a defense mechanism; certainly it violates the basic psychology of incentives to learning. Students will learn if they attempt what they are capable of learning and if they are properly motivated to learn."

This last quote was taken from a book by Williamson and Darley, *Student Personnel Work*, published in 1937 by the McGraw-Hill Book Company. In this work, they expanded on the methods and philosophy behind the Minnesota system, and their comments merit extensive quotation here. They, of course, would not still subscribe to everything here; philosophies and opinions change over a period of 30 years, and the following is not presented as current thinking, but rather to demonstrate their approach during the 1930's. However, most of it still sounds decidedly modern.

(Readers who wish to be brought up to date should consult Williamson's more recent 1962 book, *Student Personnel Services in Colleges and Universities*, also published by McGraw-Hill.)

The tenor of their approach is established in their dedication of the book to Dean J. B. Johnston, a pioneering administrator intensely interested in the problems of the student. They cite a quote from Dean Johnston on the development of a college personnel program:

---

* With an entrance test.

To discover the individual's outstanding interests, traits, and endowments, and to help him discover the function in the dynamic social order in which he will find opportunities for the exercise of his powers in a satisfying way.

The philosophy of yet another pioneer at Minnesota, D. G. Paterson, is apparent in the Introduction that Paterson prepared for the Williamson and Darley book:

The present volume departs from the orthodox vocational guidance point of view and is distinctly in line with newer conceptions subsumed under the term personnel work.

This newer approach makes use of sources of occupational information but shifts the emphasis to a study of the individual in relation to occupational adjustment—his capacities, abilities, interests, and character traits in relation to occupational requirements, as being the most practical way of providing help for youngsters faced with the necessity of wisely choosing a life work.

The newer approach could not have been developed had it not been for the small but steady progress made by psychologists in dealing with the psychology of individual mental differences. That sufficient theoretical and technological progress has now been made to warrant intensive application in this admittedly difficult field is the thesis underlying the presentation of principles, point of view, methods, and results in the following chapters.

A careful reading of the Williamson-Darley book should make clear that this newer approach to the age old problem of guidance forces the professionalization of the guidance worker in the best sense of that term. Mere knowledge of industry and of vocational information books and pamphlets is not enough. The modern personnel worker must be thoroughly grounded in psychology, in research and statistics, and in clinical procedures as well.

Some of the specific programs established to help students are described by Williamson and Darley (pp. 55, 66, 72 and 81):

At Minnesota, entering freshmen have a full schedule of freshmen-week activities. Health and psychiatric examinations are given. Entrance and special college testing programs are scheduled. Lectures on occupations, on University resources, and on study techniques are included in the program. . . . Students in need of special vocational counseling are referred to vocational counselors *before* planning their programs. Faculty representatives of the various departments and colleges help each student select his courses in an individual interview. . . .

At Minnesota, faculty counseling systems were established early in the development of personnel work to bring clinical emphasis into the use of test scores and other quantitative data available on students. D. G. Paterson began a program of student counseling in 1921 in the Arts College.

The objectives of this program were: First, to bring about a more harmonious adjustment of individual students to the opportunities available within and without the University, and second, to establish, so far as possible, the friendly and constructive personal relationship between individual members of the faculty and students desiring such contact. . . .

One general caution may be voiced regarding the personnel function of disseminating vocational information. When it is unaccompanied by any analysis of the individual, it can render little or no service in creating better vocational choices. The assumption that the student will come to know his own interests, abilities, needs, strengths, or weaknesses, by exposure to vocational information, is of course, groundless. . . .

In the direct line of evolution of student personnel work at Minnesota, the University Testing Bureau was established in 1932, by the Board of Regents, acting upon the recommendation of the Board of Admissions. At Minnesota, all personnel agencies and work dovetail with or radiate from this guidance clinic. . . . The development of this guidance clinic is one of the unique features of Minnesota's personnel work. It affords an effective means of coordinating or focusing on each student all available personnel resources; it seems also to be more effective than an enforced administrative union of the many personnel agencies on this campus.

These comments emphasize the role of the Testing Bureau as a diagnostic clinic designed to help the other offices around campus, a philosophy still adhered to today at Minnesota. Counselors at Minnesota talk to others about the student's welfare, e.g., parents, faculty members, employers, almost as frequently as they talk directly with students.

These preceding quotations relate how the Testing Bureau and related facilities came into existence; the next few give some of the philosophy behind the daily operations (pp. 82, 83 and 90):

The occurrence of irrational vocational and educational choices among college students, as well as failure to make any definite choice, is so widespread as to need little exposition. It is the exceptional student who makes his choice after an objective analysis and evaluation of his assets and liabilities. Most student choices result from the casual and often ill-advised influence of parents, classmates, or teachers; from a desire to make money or gain a position of financial and social prominence; or from romantic and superficial aspects of jobs. For a student to force himself, or to be forced, to continue in a type of academic competition which is beyond his capacity and uncongenial to his basic interests and emotional tendencies often leads to maladjustments of a serious nature. Students do not perform enthusiastically and with maximum efficiency when they undertake the wrong course, no matter how stimulating the instruction. To say that a university has no responsibility beyond the provision of instruction does not absolve it from some blame for these maladjustments. It is also a university's responsibility to provide an atmosphere which will cultivate a desire to learn. . . .

To insure satisfactory academic and vocational adjustment, it becomes necessary to subject students to a clinical procedure which utilizes and integrates methods of selection, vocational and educational orientation, and scholastic motivation. . . .

Briefly stated, this method is a combination of the measurement method of psychologists and the case method of the social workers with the added feature of continuity of case work. . . . The psychological test is given proper weight by interpreting the scores in terms of the student's entire case history. The clinical approach provides a flexibility of analysis which allows for the errors of the various analytic methods, for the dynamic character of students, and for the variability of the academic criteria for which success is measured. . . .

All data collected on the individual case by vocational testing and . . . (routine clerical questionnaires) . . . are brought to focus in the vocational counseling interview. It is primarily for this service that the Bureau operates since it is only in this capacity that intensive study is made of a student's problems and active measures taken to adjust them. . . . The Bureau's work in this field is an attempt to combine case work methods, interviews, and testing techniques into vocational counseling.

Certainly one of the most distinctive features of the Minnesota counseling point of view was (and is) the heavy reliance on standardized tests. Williamson and Darley continually stressed the value, indeed the absolute necessity, of having available objective data on the individual being counseled while, at the same time, they continually cautioned against over-interpretation of such data. Their discussions on the use of tests can frequently be split into halves, the first advocating their use, the second warning of naïve over-use (pp. 125 and 129):

> The most controversial of all counseling techniques . . . (are) the standardized tests and measuring instruments available for counseling. As is usually the case, the conflict here is not based on a clear interpretation of facts but is primarily a clash with beliefs, some of which have all the fervor of religious faith. In the first place, test makers, having turned out some tests of doubtful value, must bear a share of the blame. In the second place, a large group of workers have expected a great deal more of tests than could possibly result from the use of any measuring instrument in any field of endeavor. . . .
>
> Testing seems such an easy solution to so many problems that the difficulties inherent in testing procedures tend to be overlooked or minimized and the tests themselves appear to be grossly misused, even with the best intention on the part of the users. On the other hand, there are many who still see nothing worthwhile in tests, and have continued to pass subjective judgments. . . . In fact, one might say that the reactionaries and the enthusiasts together have so confused the basic issue of testing and mental measurement that it is difficult to take a sane middle path in discussing the problems of testing. . . .
>
> The sole purpose of testing is essentially this: to refine our impressions of a given individual and to make those impressions more accurate, and to permit the impressions to be passed on to other people who may serve the individual in the counseling capacity.

The following quotes illustrate the flavor of their extensive discussion of the use of tests in counseling (pp. 154, 159 and 160):

> Since the reliability, validity, and standards for any measuring instrument must be worked out on the local group, it should be obvious that practical use of tests should grow out of local research. While this may tend to postpone the development of a testing program in conjunction with guidance, the results gained and the accuracy and stability of measurements will well repay the delay in setting up a program. No matter what type of measuring instrument is used, the counselor must know how his own group performs on it. . . .
>
> The mere quantification of performance should not be mistaken for objectivity in measurement. Unfortunately, most of us much prefer to use these quantitative measurements of fluctuating characteristics as final judgments. Probably no greater mistake can be made than this. . . .
>
> In individual programs carried on by the clinical tester, tests of all sorts and descriptions may be used in diagnosis of individual problems. These problems may be problems of strengths or weaknesses in the individual, but their isolation depends upon careful measurement. In this work of diagnosis, achievement tests, aptitude tests, interest tests, attitude scales, special apitude tests, and every conceivable type of measurement should be drawn upon in getting a well-rounded picture of the individual's capacities and background. On the basis of such a diagnosis, it will be pos-

sible for the counselor to use the test results in differential prediction or guidance of the individual.

They were somewhat dubious about personality inventories and said (p. 155):

> We venture the opinion that so little counseling and clinical use has been made of tests of attitudes, adjustments, emotions, conduct, and ethical discrimination as to warrant the recommendation that such tests should be cautiously and critically, if at all, used as counseling tools.

The following is a sample of their comments concerning the counselor's role as test interpreter (p. 167):

> The counselor should be so far sympathetic with the student that he is able to see the problem through the student's eyes, and so far objective that he is able to recognize the errors in the student's judgment. Once the general direction toward which the student's aptitudes and interests should be oriented is tentatively determined—and we have seen that this may be done, with a certain margin of error, by means of tests and other data— the counselor must attempt to clear the student's thinking. . . . In no instance should a decision be made by the counselor without explanation to the student as to how that decision was reached. Tentative conclusions should be evolved by counselor and counseled working in cooperation. This does not mean that no prediction is made, or no advice given. But prediction and advice should follow upon explanation and persuasion. If the counselor is successful in his guidance, the student should come to see the possible solutions of his problems just as the counselor sees them. If the counselor is unsuccessful, if the advisee fails to see eye-to-eye with his adviser, it must be inferred that the counselor is not sufficiently persuasive, that some information vital to correct diagnosis is lacking, or that the counselor has attempted to develop a plan for the student which is not in harmony with all important facts of the case.

Finally, Williamson and Darley's summary of the counseling process (pp. 169, 171 and 172):

> Assume that a student has come to a counselor for educational and vocational guidance. The first step is that of *clinical analysis*. From the techniques described earlier, the counselor must select those which will best apply to the student in front of him. . . . (For example) if the student is planning to enter academic competition on the college level, it becomes advisable to determine whether he possesses . . . the minimum amount of intelligence for college level work. . . .
>
> The second step may be defined as *clinical synthesis*, or the orderly assembling of an extensive series of fact derived from a study of the individual case by every interested personnel agency. It is in this step of clinical synthesis that the counselor's diagnostic experience again comes into play, in weighing the various facts, in seeing behind test scores to their possible causes, in setting quantitative data in its proper relationship to qualitative data about the individual. . . .
>
> The third step in clinical guidance is that of *diagnosis*. Diagnosis is aimed at describing the maladjustments or problems or problem complexes. . . . This step of diagnosis is a rule rather than the exception because students tend to seek a counselor's aid only when a problem exists.
>
> The next step is that of *prognosis*, which grows naturally out of the step of diagnosis. All available evidence is summarized and presented to the stu-

dent in terms of the respective probabilities of various alternative recommendations concerning the student's occupational and educational plans. *The recommendations upon which prognoses are based must be in terms of alternatives so that the student may make his own choice.* (Italics added.)

The fifth step in our scheme of student guidance is that of *treatment*. This word has an unfortunate connotation, but we should prefer to have it stand for whatever is done by the counselor, by the student, or by the institution to put into operation a set of recommendations selected by the student. The treatment may involve questions of attitude and morale that can be handled by the counselor or others.

Always at Minnesota, there has been concern for evaluating the impact of what has been done (p. 161):

The vocational counselor must, of course, be numbered among those who find advice the easiest thing in the world to give, but it requires a good deal more courage to check up on the adequacy of this advice. . . . This evaluation is naturally relatively limited, but it is indispensable if the counselor wishes to see actual evidence of success or failure.

These quotes illustrate, albeit inadequately, the counseling climate at Minnesota during the 1930's. Three themes could be summarized:

1. The emphasis on the individual.
2. The emphasis on the use of objective data to make decisions.
3. The emphasis on the educational and vocational planning of the student.

These are the techniques that will be evaluated in the following pages.

CHAPTER FOUR

REVIEW OF THE LITERATURE

There is an ever-increasing body of evidence to show that counseling is effective in changing behavior. While the changes are never dramatic—all the counseled under-achievers don't make Phi Beta Kappa nor even graduate, all the anxious freshmen girls don't turn into sophomore queens—they are consistent and generally show that the counseled students make better grades, or are more comfortable with life, or have a more accurate perception of themselves or, in general, score higher on whatever relevant criterion the counseling researcher has chosen.

While the problem of the counseling criterion has not been solved, in some ways it has been overwhelmed by the number and diversity of criteria used by investigators. Improvement in grades, higher frequency of graduation, more involvement in social activities, better progress in post-high school endeavors, involuntary motor responses to a word association test, scores on adjustment inventories, changes in self-perception, and more accurate awareness of specific interests are some of the criteria that have been shown to be related to seeking and receiving counseling. Not all counselors agree on which of these criteria are crucial, nor should they. Counselors in different settings have different goals and it should be their decision as professional people to decide which criterion is appropriate. But the point seems clear that whenever counselors decide upon a relevant criterion, more often than not the clients show changes in the desired direction.

There are many studies to substantiate these statements, some of which are reviewed below. Because it is a crucial point in counseling research and scientific methodology in general, special attention has been given in these reviews to whether the study used a "motivated" or "non-motivated" control group, that is, whether or

14

not the control group was selected from students motivated to seek counseling, or whether it was developed in some way from other students. If the control group was a non-motivated one, the meaning of the comparison between the groups is weakened considerably. Students who are motivated to seek counseling might be motivated to act differently in other ways, and this alone might account for the differences found between counseled and non-counseled students. (This possible self-selection is considered in more detail in Chapter 5.)

STUDIES WITH NO CONTROL GROUPS

Methodologically, studies with no control groups are the weakest, especially as they have often used no criterion other than the student's self-report. However, they add useful information, usually by comparing one type, or amount, of counseling with another.

An early study by Viteles (1929) reported a follow-up of 75 out of 91 cases seen in the University of Pennsylvania Guidance Clinic during the school year 1923–1924. The trend of the differences suggested that there was more school failure among those who did not follow the advice than among those who followed it, although the number of cases in the various sub-groups was too small for significance tests. (If counselors of 40 years ago could achieve beneficial results, how much better should we be able to do today with our vastly improved measuring techniques and expanded knowledge of the world of work!)

In a unique study, Lorimer (1944) followed up 397 Columbia College students who had all been counseled by one man, Dean Herbert E. Hawkes. Dean Hawkes was apparently an avid believer in the Strong Vocational Interest Blank, and also believed in giving students direct advice. His results, measured by student self-reports, were impressive. Eighty-seven percent of the students responded; all but 11 percent agreed with the results of their conferences with Dean Hawkes and not a single student who followed his advice expressed dissatisfaction or unhappiness.

Stone and Simos (1948) reported a follow-up study on counselees from a public employment office. Half of the clients were counseled in a personal interview, the other half received a letter which summarized their test results and suggested specific training and employment possibilities. In a questionnaire sent to them 6 months later (80 percent responded), both groups expressed satisfaction with the service, although the personally counseled group reported more satisfaction.

Counselees from the University of Chicago's counseling center were asked their opinions of the services in a questionnaire study by Porter (1957). They also expressed satisfaction with the services, and those with the more interviews reported the greater satisfaction.

NON-MOTIVATED CONTROL GROUPS

The study reported in the following chapters used the non-motivated control group developed by Williamson and Bordin in their earlier study. In their original report, they showed that students who sought and received counseling earned better grades and rated higher on an adjustment rating than another group of students of equal ability who neither sought nor received counseling.

These findings have been replicated several times in different settings. Sherriffs (1949) reported that 34 students from an introductory psychology class who were given a personal interview with the instructor improved their test scores on subsequent examinations more than the remainder of the class. Those students who were rated highest on tension and need for affection and praise improved the most.

Kirchheimer, Axelrod, and Hickerson (1949) compared improvement in grades for four groups of University of California veterans classified according to whether they had received counseling and whether they had changed their course of study. Their results indicated that the counseled students improved their grades significantly more than the non-counseled, and those counseled students who changed their major (presumably as a result of the counseling) showed even more improvement.

Faries (1955) compared 140 students who took advantage of the counseling offered during an orientation course with a group of controls of equal ability. He found that 77 percent of the counseled group graduated from college as compared with 51 percent of the non-counseled group.

Ward (1948) showed that a group of counseled veterans at the University of Oregon averaged slightly higher in subsequent scholarship than a group of matched controls even though they apparently were less satisfied with their collegiate experiences.

Ivey (1962) compared a group of counseled students at Bucknell University with a random sample of non-counseled students. About half of the counseled students came of their own accord; the other half were referred by various sources. There were no differences between the counseled and non-counseled students on either CEEB scores or high school rank, indicating that, at Bucknell at least, there was no difference in scholastic aptitude between those who sought counseling and those who did not. Results from this study indicated clearly, however, that the counseled students' grades improved more than those of the non-counseled. The difference was statistically significant, roughly one-third of a standard deviation, and it was large enough to have practical significance.

An earlier study reported by Cole (1939) does not make clear whether the control group was a motivated one. To be conservative, the results will be reported in this section. In 1936 he followed up two matched groups of 100 boys who had been members of the Worcester, Massachusetts, Boys' Club in 1931. One group had been counseled, the other had not. He found the counseled group to be significantly higher on such criteria as persistence in school, job level, and freedom from delinquency, criteria that seem particularly meaningful.

A recent study by Watson (1961) compared three groups of students, all of whom had been referred for intensive counseling. One group accepted and made use of the counseling (median number of interviews, 10), the second group denied that they needed help, and the third group did not respond at all to the invitation.

Two years later the first group was distinctly superior to the other groups in scholastic achievement as measured by continued attendance in school and graduation with honors. They were also more successful in dealing with academic failure, more able to make valid decisions about withdrawal, and more often elicited favorable comments from instructors.

Not all studies show favorable results. Scarborough and Wright (1957) report no difference in grade point or proportion graduating from college between a group of students participating in a 4-day counseling clinic before entering DePauw University and a group of matched controls. Guthrie and O'Neill (1953) found no differences between groups of college students who had received different amounts of dormitory counseling.

The studies reported to this point, while almost uniformly in favor of the hypothesis of counseling effectiveness, cannot be considered definitive. The lack of an adequate control group is a serious criticism, one that cannot be erased by even dozens of studies showing results favoring counseled over non-counseled students. In the face of this evidence, however, those who hold for the third factor explaining both the student's tendency to seek counseling and earn better grades (or whatever) must start coming forward with some demonstration of that factor. These data showing the *associative connection* between counseling and various kinds of changes cannot be dismissed lightly.

MOTIVATED CONTROL GROUPS

Fortunately, the demonstrated effectiveness of counseling does not rest exclusively on studies using non-motivated controls. Several researchers have found ways to turn away clients, or at least hold them off for some period of time, for later assessment and comparison with counseled students. Several of these studies have been well done, and the results deserve study by anyone interested in counseling outcomes research.

In 1951 at the University of Minnesota, Berdie (1954) randomly divided 180 freshmen into an experimental and control group. An effort was made to counsel all of the experimental group and withhold counseling from the controls until the project was over (approximately 6 months). At the project's completion, complete data were available on 61 experimentals and 57 controls.

The results showed:

1. Very little difference in academic achievement.
2. No difference in their ability to predict their own grades.
3. Counseled men were better able to rate their own interests as measured by an interest inventory.
4. A higher percentage of control group students dropped from the University.

Berdie concluded, "This study has provided evidence that agreement between self-ratings and more objective measurements can be influenced by counseling."

Jesness (1955) also used a "delay" control group, holding them off for 2 months while the experimental group was being counseled, then retesting both groups. He found no change on nine variables, dealing mainly with the student's self-concept, designed to measure personality change. However, he did find significant differences between the two groups in the vocational planning area. He concluded, "The analysis in the specific area of vocational planning has indicated that subjects who received counseling tend to make more changes in their vocational plans and to select new vocations which were more suited to them" (p. 140).

Counseling can aid social adjustment. Freshman girls scoring low on an inventory of social adjustment were divided into two sub-groups in a series of studies by Aldrich (1942, 1949). One group was given normal counseling, the other was given more elaborate attention, including introduction into several college activities. A follow-up at the end of the year showed the group that had entered the activities had changed for the better, both in terms of ratings of adjustment and scores on the inventory.

A follow-up several years later showed that the experimental group continued to be more active in various social activities, though perhaps at the expense of their grades. The controls had achieved slightly better marks.

A series of studies conducted at the University of Minnesota during the early 1950's is summarized in Volsky, Magoon, Norman, and Hoyt (1965). In their book, an impressive attempt to deal with the theoretical and practical problems in counseling research, they report the results of an experimental study of counseling outcomes in which 80 counseled students were compared, on pre- and post-counseling measures, with 20 randomly selected control students who had sought counseling at the same time but were held off from counseling until the experiment had been completed. (As it happened, the waiting period stretched into the summer and none of the control students ever returned.)

Before this experiment was conducted, these authors spent several years developing a theoretical framework for studying change as a result of counseling, two of them completing doctoral dissertations in this area. (Hoyt, 1954; Magoon, 1954) Their work finally resulted in the conclusions that counseling should:

1. Lower the client's *anxiety* level.
2. Decrease his *defensiveness*.
3. Increase his *problem-solving abilities*.

Inventories to measure these three variables were empirically developed and validated on various student groups, then used as pre- and post-measures in the counseling effectiveness experiment.

As a result of separating the 100 subjects into sub-groups, a total of 33 hypotheses were tested.

The only result achieving statistical significance (at the .05 level) indicated that the non-counseled students improved their problem-solving ability during this period more than the counseled ones!

These results were, of course, distressing to the authors and they permitted themselves some post-facto speculation as to where their theoretical approach went wrong; they seemed to conclude that the changes attributable to counseling were unique to each student and did not show up on variables designed to measure average group trends.

Fortunately, they did not allow their over-zealous concern for theory to overwhelm their common sense, and they went ahead to report several follow-up studies on their groups for two variables of the type for which they earlier had reported disdain, i.e., grade point average and satisfactory progress toward a degree.

The results, earlier reported by Vosbeck (1959), showed the counseled students to be in better shape academically, and the pattern persisted through two subsequent follow-up studies of the students' transcripts. The grade-point data can be briefly summarized:

GRADE POINT AVERAGES

	N	Pre-Counseling	During Counseling	Post-Counseling 3 yrs.	5 yrs.	7 yrs.
Experimentals	80	2.09	2.01	2.34	2.46	2.42
Controls	20	2.07	2.00	2.09	2.16	2.27

Within the counseled group, the pre- versus post-counseling differences were significant; within the non-counseled group, they were not. However, the comparisons on the post-counseling measures between the counseled and non-counseled group were not statistically significant, leaving the interpretation somewhat in doubt, but the differences clearly favored the counseled students.

The data showing satisfactory progress in college were also in favor of the counseled students and those differences were large enough to be statistically, and practically, significant. The percentage in each group who had earned a degree or were still making satisfying progress was as follows:

	N	Post-counseling Follow-up 3 yrs.	5 yrs.	7 yrs.
Experimental sample	80	74%	72%	72%
Control sample	20	35%	40%	45%

The major contribution of this study, it seems to me, is the demonstration that real differences appear, as a result of counseling, on variables that are important to the counselor and his client, i.e., grades and academic progress, but not on the sort of theoretical constructs that are important to these theorizing researchers. Perhaps we are not yet ready for such elaborate theoretical treatments; perhaps we have far more basic hard work to do before our data merit such extensive super-structures.

In a study at Wake Forest College, Williams (1962) reported a study using both motivated and non-motivated controls. Each group contained about 40 students.

For a criterion, this study used a modification of the Butler and Haigh Q Sort to study adjustment changes. Changes in congruence among concepts of self, ideal self, and ordinary person were related to the educational-vocational counseling. The results showed that:

1. Before counseling, clients showed a lower adjustment level and less over-all concept congruence than non-clients.

2. The adjustment level and over-all concept congruence of counseled clients increased significantly more than that of either the motivated or non-motivated controls.

3. Following counseling, the adjustment level and over-all concept congruence of clients did *not* differ significantly from that of non-clients.

4. Over a 4-month follow-up period, the changes remained fairly stable.

Williams' conclusion was that educational-vocational counseling restores a normal level of adjustment and degree of congruence among the client's perceptions of himself, his ideal self, and other persons.

The basic counseling procedure for most of these Wake Forest students was "interview—testing—final interview." In two imaginative extensions of the earlier project (Williams and Hills, 1962; Hills and Williams, 1965), three further groups of students were studied, again using the S-I-O measure of self-concept as a dependent variable, to ascertain what aspects of the counseling were causing these changes.

The first group filled out the S-I-O evaluation immediately after the first interview and testing. Their scores showed that the effects of this treatment alone could not account for the changes reported in the initial study.

The second group completed the S-I-O evaluation after the first interview and testing and after receiving a written summary of their results on the tests. Their scores indicated that simply receiving test results also was not sufficient to induce the earlier reported post-counseling changes.

The third group filled out the S-I-O evaluation after going through the first interview, testing, receiving a written report, and having the final interview. Their adjustment scores were higher than either of the two groups just described and not significantly different (though slightly lower) from the post-counseling scores of the counseled group from the initial 1962 study.

Based on these results, the authors conclude, "The key to the positive self-perception changes associated with brief educational-vocational counseling seems to rest where the client-centered theorists have proposed that it does, namely, in the client-counselor interpersonal relationship" (Hills and Williams, in press).

At Duke University, Spielberger, Weitz, and Denny (1962) invited college freshmen with high anxiety scores to participate in counseling groups designed to help them to make more effective adjustments to college life. Half (N = 53) of those who volunteered were seen weekly in group counseling sessions, the other half served as a control group. Improvement in academic performance was used as the criterion.

The counseled students improved their GPA about three-fifths of a standard deviation while the controls improved less than one-quarter standard deviation. This difference was even more pronounced when the counseled group was split into high, middle, and low in terms of attendance at the counseling sessions. Among all groups motivated to seeking counseling, the amount of counseling seemed to have some impact on an objective criterion.

Golburgh and Glanz (1962) report positive results using group counseling to help students overcome difficulties in classroom recitations. Twenty-five students, all reporting this type of problem, were selected for this study. They were paired on ability scores, then randomly assigned to experimental and control groups. The measures used were teacher, self, and peer ratings, and a self-attitude questionnaire. Each of these was collected pre- and post-counseling. The counseling consisted of group sessions in which the problem of class recitations was directly approached. Gains between pre- and post-ratings measures were significantly in favor of the counseled students on the teacher and self rating and the attitude questionnaire. There was no difference on the peer rating.

The use of an objective criterion of emotional stability and a subsquent 10-year follow-up stands out in an important series of studies on a ninth grade class from a Flint, Michigan, school. This class (N = 468) was divided into two comparable halves. One half was used as a control group and received only the usual school guidance while the experimental half received intensive counseling over a 3-year period. After this, 24 from each group were tested by the Luria technique, a method of using involuntary motor responses to a word association test as an indication of emotional stability. The results showed the experimental group to be significantly more stable (Worbois, 1947). This was a very well-conducted study, and it deserves replication.

Ten years after high school graduation, these students from the Flint schools were located and studied once again. Using school records, the investigators found that 140 of the experimental group had graduated from high school versus 119 of the controls. About

240 of the original 468 were located and differences were again found in favor of the experimental group on general adjustment (as measured by the Bell Adjustment Inventory), cultural status, educational status, educational achievement, and occupational status (Cantoni, 1955).

One of the most ambitious studies of the effect of counseling was conducted by Rothney (1958). He randomly assigned 870 students from four Wisconsin high schools to experimental and control groups, then supervised counseling of the experimental group during their high school days. Two follow-up studies of the entire group were conducted, the first about 2½ years after high school graduation, the second about 5 years.

Of the original group of 870, about 690 were available for this second follow-up and Rothney reports 100 percent follow-up of this group. In his summary chapter, he reports the following results:

The experimentals:

1. achieved slightly higher academic records in high school and post-high school education;
2. indicated more realism about their own strengths and weaknesses at the time they were graduated from high school;
3. were less dissatisfied with their high school experiences;
4. had different vocational aspirations;
5. were more consistent in expression of, entering into, and remaining in their vocational choices, classified by areas;
6. made more progress in employment during the five-year period following high school graduation;
7. were more likely to go on to higher education, to remain to graduate, and to plan for continuation of higher education;
8. were more satisfied with their post-high school education;
9. expressed greater satisfaction with their status five years after high school and were more satisfied in retrospect with their post-high school experiences;
10. participated in more self-improvement activities after completing high school;
11. looked back more favorably on the counseling they had obtained.

While none of these reported differences was very large, they were consistently in the predicted direction.

Rothney concluded, "It seems clear that the differences between the counseled and comparison subjects of this study after they had graduated from high school were less than one would hypothesize in view of the claims frequently made by guidance workers. . . . There can be no doubt, however, that some important differences between the counseled and comparison groups did appear and that they could not be attributed to chance alone."

Finally, a recent work by Schofield (1963) is relevant here since it is a discussion of the field of psychotherapy and attempts to answer for that area some of the questions raised above for the

counseling area. Schofield's book, which discusses the characteristics of those who seek psychotherapy, of those who give it, and
relevant research on the outcomes, is recommended reading for
any practitioner in a helping occupation who wishes to understand
his own field better and who wants to think seriously about what
his own professional goals should be.

SUMMARY

The studies cited above illustrate the wide range of research
on counseling outcomes. From a variety of sources, utilizing a
variety of counseling philosophies, positive results have come,
pointing out that counseling does something, usually something of
value to the student. The changes are modest in magnitude, but
the consistency of the results indicate they certainly exist.

A noteworthy trend is the improvement in methods in more
recent studies. The designs are more sophisticated, the controls
more adequate, the measuring instruments more accurate, and the
time spans longer. However, considering the number of personnel
involved and the amount of funds invested in counseling functions
in various institutional settings, the *volume* of good research is still
a mere trickle. More effort is essential.

CHAPTER FIVE

HOW DO STUDENTS WHO SEEK COUNSELING DIFFER FROM THOSE WHO DO NOT?

Results in later chapters will show that the students who were counseled 25 years ago are slightly better off today than the non-counseled ones. This investigator believes that the differences are attributable to the counseling received, but others may not accept this conclusion so readily because of the inadequate design of this research.

The counseled students sought counseling, but the control students did not. This lack of a randomly selected control group was the most glaring deficiency in this project as there was the considerable danger that these were different types of people and that differences between them might be due to factors other than counseling. In particular, it might be argued that those students who sought out campus services were better adjusted, in some sense, than the average student. If so, this alone could explain the findings; the counseling would be extraneous.

Before trying to ascertain if this was the case, a further point should be made. In comparing students who seek counseling with those who do not, one of three situations may exist:

1. Those who seek counseling may be *better* in some sense (brighter, better adjusted, higher socioeconomic status, or the like).
2. The two groups may be *alike*.
3. The students who seek counseling may be *worse*.

The results of the current research are jeopardized only if the first of these alternatives is true. To establish the efficacy of the

25

current design, it is not necessary to show that the counseled and non-counseled students were alike before counseling, but only that the counseled students were not better. If, in fact, the counseled students were initially worse, the results reported later are even more dramatic.

Two methods have been employed to determine if the differences between the groups existed before counseling or whether they were created by counseling. First, pre-counseling data from counseled and non-counseled students have been analyzed. Second, an attempt has been made to establish some causal connection between the counseling and the student's subsequent actions. For example, if the counseling had any effect, counseled students should end up in occupations more consonant with their measured interests than non-counseled students.

Pre-counseling Differences between Counseled and Non-counseled Students

Schneidler-Berdie Sample

An earlier study is highly relevant as it dealt with a population closely similar to the one in the present study. Schneidler and Berdie (1942) compared counseled and non-counseled students, before counseling, from the 1939 SLA freshman class at the University of Minnesota. They reported comparisons between the two groups on the following variables:

High school grades
College entrance examination (1937 ACE)
Cooperative English Test
Mathematics Achievement Test
Natural Science Achievement Test
Social Sciences Achievement Test
Minnesota Personality Scale
Strong Vocational Interest Blank

The data showed virtually no differences between the students who sought counseling and those who did not. Of the differences, only a few achieved statistical significance and none was of practical importance, especially since the differences were not consistently in the same direction. Schneidler and Berdie concluded that, on these variables, the two groups were virtually identical.

A Random Sample from 1933–1936 University Files

For a second comparison, a random sample, with the same

composition of sex and year of entry as the Williamson-Bordin group, was drawn from University files by using entering freshman registration lists. This sample was split into counseled and non-counseled groups for comparison on High School Rank (HSR) and College Aptitude Test (CAT) percentile. Those data are listed in Table 1.

TABLE 1. *Comparison of a Random Sample of Counseled versus Non-counseled Students on High School Rank and College Aptitude Test Percentile*

	HSR			CAT Percentile		
	N	Mean	S.D.	N	Mean	S.D.
Counseled	290	69.70	23.54	304	57.59	26.72
Non-counseled	436	67.11	25.17	465	56.94	26.70

The differences, slightly in favor of the counseled group, are neither statistically nor practically significant.

BALLER UNIVERSITY OF NEBRASKA SAMPLE

Baller (1944) compared counseled and non-counseled students at the University of Nebraska and reports: "Clearly, the program of guidance tests has appealed more to the abler students." His comparisons are reported in terms of scaled scores, and while it is difficult to estimate the magnitude of the differences, they clearly exist. Baller further reports that those students seeking counseling mainly for educational-vocational planning made better grades than non-counseled students. But students seeking counseling because of personal problems, although still above average on the aptitude tests, made distinctly poorer grades.

These differences found at the University of Nebraska seem to differ somewhat from the data from the University of Minnesota indicating, as Baller wisely pointed out, "The way in which such a service is accepted by students in one university cannot safely be assumed to characterize another student population."

BERDIE-HOOD SAMPLE

Data on students currently enrolled at Minnesota were also examined. Most of the members of the 1961 SLA freshmen class at Minnesota were participants in a state-wide questionnaire study conducted by Berdie and Hood (1963) while those students were Minnesota high school seniors. The information collected covered socioeconomic level, future plans, and also included several personality items. For each of these students, results were also available on the MMPI taken during college orientation, and the usual measures used for admission, i.e., a scholastic ability test and their high school rank.

During the fall of 1963, two years after these students had entered college, the files of the Student Counseling Bureau were examined to determine which of these students had sought counseling. Two groups, one counseled, the other not, were compared on all of the available data to see what differences may have existed before these students sought counseling. (About 20 percent of the group had been counseled by this time.)

Table 2 gives comparative data on the two groups on several aptitude measures.

TABLE 2. *Aptitude Data on 1961 SLA Freshmen: Counseled versus Non-counseled*

	Male				Female			
	Counseled		Non-counseled		Counseled		Non-counseled	
	Mean (N = 204)	S.D.	Mean (N = 947)	S.D.	Mean (N = 196)	S.D.	Mean (N = 1000)	S.D.
High school rank	73.02	19.95	71.03	20.07	82.51	14.51	78.52	17.00
Minnesota Scholastic Aptitude Test	45.59	12.97	43.43	11.73	46.92	13.72	44.67	11.78
Cooperative English Test	158.91	26.85	154.16	25.77	172.21	24.00	170.90	22.45

These findings are similar to those from the random sample discussed, although in this sample, because of the large numbers in each group, the differences were statistically significant. While none of them was large, the pattern of differences consistently showed the counseled group to be mildly superior. The counseled students seem to come from a slightly different population group.

The Berdie-Hood group of students also responded to several personality items included in the questionnaire. These items, taken from the Minnesota Counseling Inventory, were those most likely to discriminate between students planning to go on to college and students making other post-high school plans.

Berdie and Hood (1963, p. 62) have the following discussion of these items:

> The questionnaire contained 25 personality inventory items from the Minnesota Counseling Inventory (MCI). Thirteen of these items were the most discriminating items from the social relations scale and 12 from the conformity scale. Scores on the social relations scale refer to the nature of the student's relations with other people. Students with low scores are generally gregarious and appear to be happy and comfortable with others. Usually they have good social skills. Students with high scores tend to be socially inept and unhappy and uncomfortable with groups of peers or adults.

The conformity scale was derived from the psychopathic deviate scale of the Minnesota Multiphasic Personality Inventory (MMPI). Students with low scores usually are reliable and responsible. Although not necessarily docile or overly submissive, they understand the need for behavior codes and social organization. Students with high scores are likely to be irresponsible, impulsive, and rebellious. They tend to be individualistic, self-centered, and some have juvenile court records.

They found some differences between groups on these items. In general, girls were more sociable than boys, and boys more often reported trouble with authorities. Between the college-goer and non-college-goer, they found "the students contemplating college indicated they saw themselves as being more sociable, they expressed less shyness, and they indicated they had fewer conflicts with family and authorities."

TABLE 3. *Percentage of Counseled and Non-counseled Students Answering "True" to Certain Personality Items*

Social Relations Items	Male		Female	
	Counseled (N = 204)	Non-counseled (N = 947)	Counseled (N = 196)	Non-counseled (N = 1000)
I meet strangers easily	74	77	74	77
I get along as well as the average person in social activities	92	95	93	97
I feel self-conscious when reciting in class	43	40	50	44
I feel at ease with people	79	83	79	84
I have difficulty in starting a conversation with a person who has just been introduced	39	36	35	27
I enjoy speaking before groups of people	36	33	31	30
I am rather shy in contacts with people	24	26	32	26
I enjoy entertaining people	68	64	63	77
I like to meet new people	89	87	94	95
I dislike social affairs	10	11	6	4
I find it easy to express my ideas	66	63	54	54
I avoid people when it is possible	12	11	8	6
I stay in the background at parties or social gatherings	22	23	28	15
Conformity Items				
In school I sometimes have been sent to the principal for cutting up	27	21	3	5
I am sure I get a raw deal from life	1	3	2	1
At times I have very much wanted to leave home	34	30	35	32
I find it hard to keep my mind on a task or job	22	21	24	18
My parents have often objected to the kind of people I go around with	11	10	8	6
No one seems to understand me	7	9	10	6
My family does not like the work I have chosen or the work I intend to choose for my life work	2	3	5	3
My parents and family find more fault with me than they should	19	13	10	9
If people had not had it in for me I would have been much more successful	1	1	0	0
I wish I were not so shy	34	31	34	31
I have had very peculiar and strange experiences	28	30	28	24

For these students, the percent response to each item, tabulated by counseled versus non-counseled, is listed in Table 3.

There were few notable differences between the groups, but
the trend seems unmistakably clear. With only a few exceptions,
there was a higher percentage of counseled students selecting the
"poorly adjusted" response, but there is not much excitement in a
trend that depends exclusively on percentage differences of 2, 3,
or 4 percent. The most reasonable conclusion is that there were
essentially no differences between these groups on these dimensions.

A more substantial test of the personality characteristics of
these two groups was possible since their results were available for
the Minnesota Multiphasic Personality Inventory (MMPI). In
1962 each entering freshman in SLA at Minnesota completed this
during freshman orientation.

First, the mean profile for each group was calculated; Table 4

TABLE 4.   *MMPI Profiles for Counseled and Non-counseled Males*

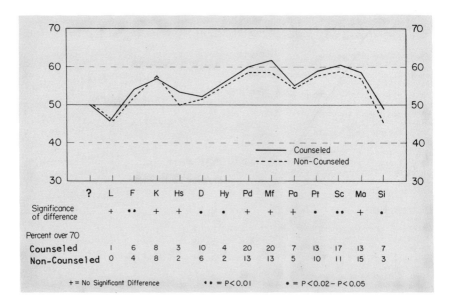

shows results for the men, and Table 5, for the women. The profiles were analyzed in a second manner by tabulating the percentage of each group with T-scores above 70. A score of 70 is two
standard deviations above the mean and usually indicates more
severe emotional problems. These percentages are also shown in
Tables 4 and 5.

The trend was again clear. Though the differences were small

Table 5. *MMPI Profiles for Counseled and Non-counseled Females*

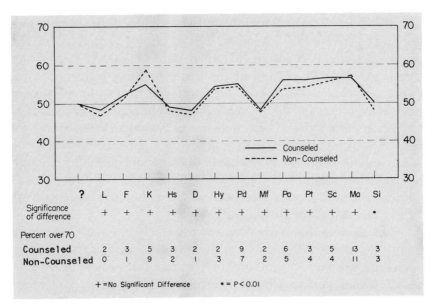

they consistently, with the exception of the K and Ma scales, showed the counseled students to be more psychologically uncomfortable. (Some investigators have hypothesized that a moderately high K may actually be a sign of *better* psychological functioning, so this reversal is perhaps not crucial.)

In all of these data, there is little support for the contention that students who seek counseling are different from those who do not, and clear rebuttal of the position that those seeking counseling are better adjusted. Clearly, this group of counseled students, before counseling, contained more students with potential personal problems than did the group of non-counseled students.

In addition to the personality variables, the counseled and non-counseled students from the Berdie-Hood sample were compared on the following items:

> Urban versus rural residence
> Number of books in home
> Number whose parents owned their own home
> Student's report of adequacy of parents' income
> Post-high school plan
> Factors influencing their selection of post-high school plan
> Amount of family financial support in college
> Parental feelings toward student's attending college
> Occupational status of father

Educational level of parents

Number of close friends planning to attend college

Virtually no differences were found. In those cases in which some trend was barely discernible, it was usually in the same direction as the data reported earlier. For example, 77 percent of the counseled students reported that their parents wanted them to go to college versus 81 percent of the non-counseled. Fifteen percent of the counseled students said they would receive no financial help from their parents in college, while 14 percent of the non-counseled students reported this. These data are hardly worth reporting, yet they do indicate the usual magnitude of difference between the groups and illustrate the faint thread of consistency running through the data. Essentially, there were no differences between the groups but, where any differences were found, the counseled students were slightly less at ease with life.

One modest difference was found which has some relevance to later discussions. In answer to the question "If you are planning on college, are you considering any graduate or professional training after your undergraduate college work?" a higher percentage of the counseled group said, "Yes"—63 versus 52 percent of the boys, 37 versus 28 percent of the girls. Later on it will be shown that the incidence of counseling is higher among advanced degree earners than among average college students. Apparently, this difference shows up even in the high school years.

WILLIAMSON-BORDIN SAMPLE

In collecting the data for the current study, some attempt was made to study differences between the counseled and non-counseled groups that might have existed before they entered the University. In the 1962 questionnaire they were asked about their parents' economic status, about how they felt toward their home

TABLE 6. *Counseled and Non-counseled Students' Descriptions of Feelings Toward Childhood Home Environment*

"When you were growing up, how would you describe your feelings toward your family and home situation?" (Check one)	Counseled	Non-counseled
I was very happy with the way things were	21.2	28.0
I was happier than average	25.3	23.6
About average	37.3	38.8
I was more unhappy than average	11.4	7.2
I was very unhappy	4.1	2.4

TABLE 7. *Counseled and Non-counseled Students' Descriptions of Parents' Economic Status*

"How would you describe your parents' economic status in comparison with that of your classmates' parents?" (Check one)

	Counseled	Non-counseled
Very much poorer	5.7	5.2
Poorer	22.1	24.8
About average	57.8	51.6
Fairly well-off	11.7	15.6
Well-to-do	2.2	2.0

situation when they were growing up, and about major disruptions in their life when they were young, such as parents' death or divorce. In addition, a fair amount of background information was collected from each person, such as parents' education, number of siblings, and so forth.

A few mild differences, shown in the following tables, did appear, but hardly any of them were either of statistical or practical significance. Any trend that did appear usually indicated, as before, that the counseled group probably had more troubles before counseling than did the control group. For example, between birth and 2 years of age, 4.4 percent of the counseled versus 1.2 percent of the control group had some severe disruption in their life when disruption was defined as one or both parents dying, or parental divorce or separation. After age 2, the percentages were virtually identical in each group.

Tables 6 and 7 give results of questions asked about their feelings toward their home situation.

Of all the pre-counseling comparisons made on this sample, this showed the strongest trend. There was the usual mild trend showing that the counseled students were more *unhappy* while they were growing up and, in this instance, the trend was supported

TABLE 8. *Counseled and Non-counseled Students' Reports of Parental Support for their Education*

"Did your parents think it was important for you to get a college education?" (Check one)

	Counseled	Non-counseled
Thought it extremely important	63.5	65.2
Thought it was all right	28.1	29.2
They were neutral	6.5	4.0
They were somewhat opposed to the idea	1.9	1.6
They were very opposed to the idea	1.1	0.4

by statistical significance at a respectable level ($2 = 9.99$, $p < .06$), though the practical difference was again slight.

We asked them about their parents' feelings toward their education. As the data in Table 8 show, again the groups were virtually identical. In this table the faint trend in the table was in favor of the non-counseled students.

Each of these groups reported the education level of their parents, and those data are presented in Table 9; again, no trend.

TABLE 9.   *Parents' Educational Level of Counseled and Non-counseled Students*

	Mother		Father	
	Counseled	Non-counseled	Counseled	Non-counseled
Less than H.S. graduate	40.0	43.2	42.0	43.6
High school graduate	22.1	22.4	12.5	15.6
Some college or business school	20.7	26.0	21.0	16.8
College graduate	16.1	8.4	22.9	22.4

Significant differences were found on one other measure, birth order. Schacter (1959) has pointed out that first-born and only children are more apt to seek out the company of others when they are under stress. From these findings, one would expect first-born and only children to seek counseling more often than the later born. This proved to be true; Table 10 shows those tabulations.

TABLE 10.   *First Born versus Later Born in the Counseled and Control Groups*

	First Born		Later Born	
	N	Percent	N	Percent
Counseled	210	58	154	42
Control	114	46	136	54

$$\chi^2 = 8.70 \quad p < .01$$

Just what influence this result has on the results to be reported later is not clear. First-borns were compared with the later borns on all of the various measures of success and achievement to be reported in later chapters, and no significant differences were found. Nor was any difference found in the percent of each group seeing a psychiatrist or clinical psychologist as adults.

Several other comparisons were made between the Williamson-Bordin counseled and non-counseled groups and none of these showed even the small differences found on the above questions. These other variables were:

1. Source of financial support while in college.
2. Type of residence while in college.
3. Number of siblings.
4. Number of siblings who were college graduates.
5. Family religion.

CAUSAL CONNECTIONS BETWEEN COUNSELING AND SUBSEQUENT BEHAVIORS

A further type of evidence is available on this issue of whether current differences are the result of the counseling or simply of the non-random selection of the two groups. If counseling was effective, then certain causal chains should be apparent between the counseling and the individual's action. For example, if the counseling had any effect on the student's plans, then in answer to the question "What influenced you in choosing your occupation?" the counseled student's answer should reflect this in some way. In answer to that question, the following differences were noted:

	Counseled	Non-counseled
I selected my occupation on the basis of some counseling I received	6.3 percent	0.4 percent
I selected it because I was interested in it	40.9	29.9
I went into a family business	13.2	17.4
I had always planned it	2.5	6.2

Though these differences were not large, all except the third one were statistically significant, and all fit into the framework of counseling effectiveness.

A more extensive section on the influences affecting career choices of the two groups can be found in Chapter 9 which reports the counselee's opinions of his counseling 25 years later. The answers clearly fit into the framework of counseling effectiveness since, according to the student's self-report, the counselor frequently had some impact on the student's future career.

This one area—influences surrounding vocational choice—seemed to show consistent differences between the counseled and non-counseled, both before and after counseling. Besides the questions already discussed, a further question showing differences was:

When did you decide on your current type of work?
before —
while —
after — attending undergraduate college?
The percentage of counseled students selecting each was 12

percent, 18 percent and 53 percent, respectively; for the non-counseled, 18 percent, 16 percent, and 43 percent. Thus, it appears that the non-counseled students made their career choice earlier in life. Among the graduate men, the trend was even more pronounced, as 36 percent of the non-counseled versus 14 percent of the counseled said they had decided on their career before entering college. Many times these were individuals who had decided early that they were going to be a doctor or a lawyer or something similar, then went ahead and did it. There was little indecision in their career plans and they never felt the need for counseling.

While these causal links between the counseling and the student's action are not well enough established to be overwhelmingly persuasive, that they exist at all provides some support for the hypothesis of counseling effectiveness. Those critics who say that there is some third factor operating in the student to explain both his seeking counseling and his better adjustment must also add, "and it (the third factor) has the same influence on his career plans that effective counseling would have."

A "BETTER" CONTROL GROUP

Perhaps the best data available on the adequacy of this study's design were generated by fortuitous circumstances. About one-sixth (N = 62) of the original control group sought counseling at the Student Counseling Bureau some time after the original study. For this sub-group, both pre- and post-counseling measures were available. Thus, this group can be used as a "better" control group for comparison with students already counseled and students never counseled.

If counseling was effective, these "better" control students, before they were counseled, should be like other *control* students; after counseling, they should resemble other *counseled* students. To determine this, three comparisons were made:

> **Before Counseling.** The "better" controls were compared with the remaining controls.
> **Before Counseling.** The differences between the "better" controls and their matched counseled mates were compared to the differences between the remaining controls and their matched counseled mates.
> **After Counseling.** The "better" controls were compared with both their counseled mates and the remaining controls.

To support the hypothesis that counseling was effective, the first two comparisons should show that, before counseling, the "better" controls were like the remaining controls while the third comparison should show that these "better" controls, after counseling, changed to resemble the other counseled students.

Table 11 illustrates the results of the matching on high school rank and college entrance tests. The groups are virtually identical on these variables.

For pre-counseling measures, the groups were compared on the Williamson-Bordin adjustment rating, a subjective rating based on their adjustment to the University, and first quarter grade point

TABLE 11. *Comparison of "Better" Controls and Their Experimental Mates*

	N	High School Rank		College Aptitude Test Percentile	
	N	M	S.D.	M	S.D.
"Better" controls	62	68.5	25.3	65.8	24.3
Matched experimentals	62	69.2	25.1	65.0	24.6

TABLE 12. *Comparison of Adjustment Ratings of Counseled and Control Pair Members*

			Rating of Non-counseled Control Member										
		A		B		C		D		E		TOTALS	
		N	%	N	%	N	%	N	%	N	%	N	%
Rating of Counseled Member	A	77	(25)	26	(8)	7	(2)	21	(7)	8	(3)	139	(44)
	B	37	(12)	38	(12)	8	(3)	30	(10)	3	(1)	116	(37)
	C	5	(2)	4	(1)	2	(1)	3	(1)	1	(0)	15	(5)
	D	9	(3)	12	(4)	1	(0)	9	(3)	4	(1)	35	(11)
	E	0	(0)	2	(1)	1	(0)	5	(2)	1	(0)	9	(3)
TOTALS		128	(41)	82	(26)	19	(6)	68	(22)	17	(5)	314	(100)

Number in diagonal cells = 127 (41 percent)
Number above diagonal (favoring counseled member) = 111 (35 percent)
Number below diagonal (favoring non-counseled member) = 76 (24 percent)

			Rating of "Better" Control Member										
		A		B		C		D		E		TOTALS	
		N	%	N	%	N	%	N	%	N	%	N	%
Rating of Counseled Member	A	8	(13)	8	(13)	2	(3)	4	(6)	0	(0)	22	(35)
	B	5	(8)	12	(19)	1	(2)	4	(6)	2	(3)	24	(39)
	C	0	(0)	2	(3)	0	(0)	1	(2)	0	(0)	3	(5)
	D	0	(0)	9	(15)	0	(0)	1	(2)	1	(2)	11	(18)
	E	0	(0)	1	(2)	1	(2)	0	(0)	0	(0)	2	(3)
TOTALS		13	(21)	32	(52)	4	(6)	10	(16)	3	(5)	62	(100)

Number in diagonal cells = 21 (33 percent)
Number above diagonal (favoring counseled member) = 23 (37 percent)
Number below diagonal (favoring non-counseled member) = 18 (30 percent)

average (GPA; A = 4.0, etc.). For a post-counseling measure, the groups were compared on frequency of graduation.

Table 12 gives the necessary data for the comparison of these groups on the adjustment rating. This rating was made during the Williamson-Bordin study after the counseled students, but before the control students, had been to the Bureau. It was a five-point rating, running from A to E, with A indicating the best adjustment. For a more detailed description of these ratings, see Williamson and Darley (1937, pp. 262–266).

To compare the "better" controls with the remaining controls, the column totals in the top half of the table were compared with the column totals in the bottom half. There were some differences (chi-square = 17.32, df = 4, p < .01), mainly in the A and B ratings, with the non-counseled controls rating higher. This, of course, was not damaging to the hypothesis of counseling effectiveness as it indicated again that students who do not seek counseling are in slightly better shape than those who do.

To determine if the "better" controls, before counseling, were as different from their matched counseled mates as the other controls were from theirs, all of the cell frequencies in the top half of the table were compared with the analogous frequencies in the bottom half. Simple inspection indicates that the tables are similar with a few exceptions. For a more rigorous test, chi-squares were calculated for each table, using only the non-diagonal cells. This allowed for the correlation between the groups created by the original matching and gave an index of counseling effectiveness. If the counseling was effective, there should be more pairs tallied above the diagonal where the counseled member of the pair received a better rating than the control member. The Williamson-Bordin analysis has already shown this to be true, but the question crucial at this moment is whether this trend is similar in both halves of the table.

The chi-square calculation used the average of the two mirror image cells as the expected frequency in each of those two individual cells. For example, the average of the AE and EA cells frequencies was the expected value in the AE and EA cells. (It was necessary to collapse the bottom half of the table into a 3×3 matrix to avoid low expected frequencies.) For the top half of the table, chi-square = 25.56, df = 10, p < .01. For the bottom half, chi-square = 8.04, df = 3, .01 < p < .02. Both of these were statistically significant at a respectable level, and both favored the counseled groups over the control groups.

One more inspectional approach was to compare, for each matrix, the frequencies in the diagonal cells, the frequencies in the cells above the diagonal where the counseled member received the higher rating of the pair, and the frequencies in the cells below the diagonal where the control member received the higher rating. These frequencies are reported in each half of the table and, again, they show similar patterns.

These data support the contention that students who will eventually seek counseling are as different from students who have been counseled as students who will never seek counseling. Again, they offer no support to the argument that students who seek out counseling are better adjusted than those who do not.

The same comparisons can be made in a simpler manner, using first quarter GPA for these groups. Williamson and Bordin reported that the over-all control group GPA was 1.97, that of the experimental group 2.18, a difference significant at the .01 level. The same comparison between the "better" controls and their matched experimental mates was 1.98 to 2.07, a difference also significant at the .01 level. Note that the over-all control group average was 1.97; the "better" control group average was 1.98, an insignificant difference.

Again the trend was clear. The "better" controls, before they were counseled, were more like the other controls than they were like the other counseled students. The crucial question now becomes: after counseling, did they change to resemble the counseled students?

The post-counseling measure used here was frequency of graduation. While this is by no means a perfect criterion of counseling effectiveness, it has some relevance. Once a student has been admitted to the University, most counselors try to guide him to a curriculum in which he will be happy and productive, and this is certainly related to eventual graduation.

Frequency of graduation also has the considerable virtue of objectivity. The problems of reliability and validity of ratings are eliminated and almost everyone will accept this as a desirable outcome of counseling, at least when given to students of college level abilities. This serves to emphasize the importance of this final comparison.

The graduation data in Table 13 show that the desired outcome occurred. After counseling, "better" controls resembled their experimental matchmates more closely than they did the other controls.

The percentage of graduating non-counseled controls was significantly lower (at the .05 level) than either of the counseled groups; the difference between the latter two was not significant.

The "better" controls now—after counseling—resemble other

TABLE 13. *Graduation Frequencies*

	N	Percentage Graduating
"Better" controls	62	60
Matched counseled students	62	58
Remaining controls	314	47

counseled students more than they do the remaining controls. This was not true of the pre-counseling data, and seems to point to a true effect of counseling rather than a type of behavior connected with seeking out counseling.

Even with the above data in hand, this conclusion may prove too strong for some readers. But at the very least, the results indicate that desirable changes occurred during the time period when the students were being counseled.

SUMMARY

Four main trends have emerged from these studies of students who seek counseling and those who do not.

First, all of the differences between these groups were small, seldom of statistical significance (even though many of these studies used samples of several hundreds) and of dubious practical significance.

Second, the small differences on aptitude measures usually favored the counseled group. The Baller study, the random sample of the 1930's at Minnesota, and the 1961 freshman class all showed differences in favor of those seeking counseling.

Third, there was a significant difference in the birth order of the two groups, with first-born and only children being found more often in the counseled group.

Fourth, there was a clear, consistent (and small) trend for the counseled students to exhibit more personal discomfort on a variety of measures.

Perhaps the best summary of this section is to repeat the statement made earlier:

There is little support here for the contention that students who seek counseling are much different from those who do not, and clear rebuttal of the position that those seeking counseling are better adjusted.

For the current study, from the research design standpoint, these findings are reassuring. The first suggested difference, that of ability level, was controlled in the original Williamson-Bordin study because each counseled student was matched with a non-counseled student of equal ability. Thus, none of the current differences can be explained by differences in ability.

While it is difficult to evaluate the impact of the birth order phenomenon, it did not seem to affect the criteria used in this study. The first and later born groups were compared on a variety of measures, and other than this propensity to seek out counseling, hardly any other differences were found. As demonstrated in other studies, the first-borns performed slightly better on the aptitude measures, but no differences on any of the achievement or satisfaction variables were found. And, surprisingly, no difference was found in their responses to the question, "Have you ever gone to a psychologist or psychiatrist?" Sixteen percent of each group said yes. While birth order was a confounding variable, it seemed to have little impact on the outcomes of counseling.

The third faint difference, that of emotional stability and comfort, favored the non-counseled student. Any flaw in this research design probably worked against the hypothesis of counseling effectiveness. If the counseled students turn out no better than—but just as good as—the non-counseled students, an argument could be made that the counseling helped.

CHAPTER SIX

METHODOLOGY

Williamson and Bordin, in their research, selected a group of approximately 400 students who had come to the University of Minnesota Student Counseling Bureau before November 1st of their freshman year, during the years 1933 to 1936, to consult with a counselor about educational, vocational, or other personal problems. They were designated *the experimental group* and selected solely on the basis of having complete counseling case folders. One year later, these students were matched individually with other non-counseled students on college entrance test score, English proficiency test score, high school rank, age, sex, size and type of high school, and college class. The second group was *the control group*. All students were registered in the College of Science, Literature, and the Arts (SLA). There were 384 pairs, 768 students in the final sample.

Both groups were interviewed roughly one year after counseling (range = 1 to 4 years; mode = 1 year) and rated on a scale called "adjustment" which centered mainly around educational-vocational progress. The two groups were also compared on first quarter grade point average.

The results showed that:

1. The counseled students rated significantly higher on the adjustment scale.
2. The counseled students earned significantly better grades than non-counseled students—2.18 to 1.97, respectively (on a 4-point scale).

In 1961–1962, the data from this study were resurrected, and an attempt was made to locate these individuals to assess the effects of counseling over a 25-year period.

Surprisingly, virtually all of these former students were located, 761 of the 768. Of these, 731 were still alive and each of them was asked to do four things. Those four tasks and the percentage completing each were (see Table 14 for a detailed breakdown):

1. Complete a detailed 30-page questionnaire   84 percent
2. Have an hour interview   90
3. Complete the Strong Vocational Interest Blank   84
4. Take the University of Minnesota's current entrance examination   87
5. All four of the above   80
6. At least one of the above   92

INFORMATION COLLECTED

The information requested from them was concerned primarily with their achievements and their satisfaction with their job and general station in life.

Specifically, the questionnaire contained items dealing with the following areas (see copy in Appendix):

1. Educational achievements
2. College extra-curricular activities
3. Parents' status
4. Their children and spouses
5. Current occupation and job history
6. Job and occupational satisfaction
7. Awards and honors won
8. Organizational participation
9. Income and economic status
10. Recreational activities
11. Health

Most of the questions were multiple choice or completion types requiring only short answers. This questionnaire was administered through the mail, and a copy of the Strong Vocational Interest Blank was sent along at the same time.

The interview, though it was highly structured, contained mostly open-end questions which gave the individual a broad opportunity to express himself.

It covered the following areas (see copy in Appendix):

1. General questions about collegiate experiences
2. Influences on occupational choice
3. Their opinion of the counseling they had received
4. Their evaluation of their own abilities and interests
5. For the women, the effects of working on their family
6. Career plans of their children
7. Educational and emotional problems of their children
8. The individual's social life
9. Political activities

10. Marital happiness
11. Any personal problems
12. General satisfaction with life
13. Future goals

This interview was conducted in a highly systematic manner through a specified series of questions in an interview booklet. The interviewer, usually a graduate student in psychology from a nearby university, read the questions in a pre-determined order to the subject and made short notes on the booklet, condensing the individual's answer. Though it was highly structured, the interview was not an impersonal, sterile interchange. Much thought went into the arrangement of the questions to lead to the greatest possible rapport between the subject and the interviewer, and some attempt was made in hiring interviewers to select those with some social sensitivity.

The interview started with common-place questions, such as, "What is your occupation?"; proceeded through a series of innocuous questions, "Why did you decide to go to college?"; and gradually worked into the personal areas, "What personal attributes are you most proud of?" "Which ones stand in your way?" "What is the best thing about your marriage?" . . . "the worst thing?"

One index of the success of the question arrangement and the interviewer quality was that not a single participant refused to continue to the end of the interview, once it had been started. We had expected that some small percentage of people would refuse to continue when the questions became very personal, but that did not happen in a single instance. From this we assume that rapport must have been at least minimally adequate. (On a more informal note, several of these interviews were pleasant for both parties. Frequently, the interviewer was asked to stay for coffee or a drink or, occasionally, even for dinner.)

In most cases, the interviewer also administered the Minnesota Scholastic Aptitude Test during the interview. As will be discussed later, it was administered to others in groups.

After completion of the interview, each person was rated by the interviewer on several scales. (See Rating Form in the Appendix.)

All of the above data were categorized, coded appropriately, and punched into IBM cards for the analyses in this report.

While most of the questionnaire material was easily coded, this was not true of the information gained from the interview. For example, a typical interview question was "What are your main criticisms of the University currently?" This elicited a variety of answers which had to be organized in some manner. After inspection of several dozen interview booklets, categories were arbitrarily defined. While these categories should not be taken as fixed, immutable entities, usually they represent the general themes of the answers fairly well.

Of course this categorization did throw away some information and destroyed the unique flavor of the comments. For example, two of the answers to the question about current criticisms of the University were:

> My main criticism is that they won't let the Minnesota Vikings football team use their stadium.
> My main criticism of the University is that they are teaching evolution over there.

Both of these were unique, and it is unfortunate that they had to be buried in the "Other" category.

One further type of information was used in this project. About 5 percent of the individuals refused to reveal any information whatsoever about themselves. In those cases, information on their occupation and general level of achievement was gathered from a variety of sources—any that we could find available—for use in the "contribution to society" rating to be discussed later.

In addition to the current information described above, some data were available on each individual from his University records, such as his scholastic performance, honors won, high school rank, and score on college entrance test. Also, from the earlier Williamson-Bordin study, an adjustment rating was available and, for the counseled students, some psychometric measures as well as counseling case notes were in the files.

FINAL SAMPLE USED

The original Williamson-Bordin study used 384 pairs of students. In this follow-up study, several of these pairs were unavailable for a variety of reasons. Thirty people had died, seven could not be located and about 10 percent would not cooperate. In another 62 cases, the control member of the pair had since come to the Counseling Bureau for guidance, which meant that these pairs could not be used in the counseled versus non-counseled comparisons.

Because these disruptions occurred in over 100 pairs, the final analyses were done by counseled versus non-counseled groups rather than by pairs. This allowed the use of the pairs where both students had been counseled. A further advantage was that these group comparisons were computationally simpler than the pair by pair analysis. Of course, some statistical power was lost by not using the matched pair procedure, but this power loss was offset to some degree by the inclusion of over 200 people whose records would otherwise have been discarded.

For a few analyses in which it seemed particularly appropriate, the matched pair technique was used.

The total numbers in each group varied slightly, depending on the information used. Table 14 reports the percent by group and by sex who furnished each of the requested documents.

TABLE 14. *Number of Counseled and Non-counseled Returning Each Type of Information*

	Counseled			Non-counseled			Total
	Male	Female	Total	Male	Female	Total	
Initial number	238	216	454	159	155	314	768
Dead	14	4	18	9	3	12	30
Not located	4	2	6	0	1	1	7
Total available for data collection	220	210	430	150	151	301	731
Information furnished	N %	N %	N %	N %	N %	N %	N %
Questionnaire	177 80	190 90	367 85	127 85	123 82	250 83	617 84
Interview	191 87	197 94	388 90	135 90	131 87	266 88	654 90
MSAT	184 84	190 90	374 87	134 89	126 83	260 86	634 87
SVIB	175 80	188 90	363 84	127 85	122 81	249 83	612 84

In brief, the subjects in this study had been college students during the 1930's in the liberal arts college of a large, midwestern state university. When studied, they were about 45 years of age, predominantly college-educated (about half of them received a degree from Minnesota and another 15 percent earned a degree elsewhere) and, almost without exception, were urban dwellers.

About half of them lived in the Twin Cities area (Minneapolis–St. Paul), another sixth in Los Angeles. The rest were scattered through other American cities, with notable concentrations in Chicago, New York, and Washington, D.C. A small percentage lived in small towns, and an even smaller percentage, 1 or 2 percent, lived in rural areas. One percent lived outside of the United States.

LOCATING 99 PERCENT 25 YEARS LATER

One of the most successful phases of this study was the data collection portion. Ninety-nine percent of the individuals from the original study were located, and over 90 percent of those still living participated in the current study. This section reports the methods used in achieving those results. Because it may prove helpful to other investigators planning long-term follow-ups, considerable detail is given.

Locating the subjects was the first problem. Initially, no current information was available although there was some information from 25 years ago: address in student directory, University transcript address, parents' name and address, whether or not they graduated from the University and, if so, major area and degree earned.

Some people were located simply by inspecting the list of names. Freshmen of the University of Minnesota from 25 years ago have, as a group, done well, and a few have been spectacular successes. One man is now a prominent national political figure; two are well-known athletic coaches. These were located easily; others came harder.

First, the names were sent to the University alumni office and also compared with the listings in the Twin Cities phone directories. Through these sources, current addresses were found for 33 percent of the group.

Letters were mailed to these people, one over the signature of O. Meredith Wilson, President of the University, and another signed by the project directors, telling them of plans for a rather elaborate survey of freshmen of their era and asking for their cooperation. After they had returned an enclosed postal card to verify their address, a complete roster of the sample was sent to them with a note asking for their help in locating the missing people.

This was a very profitable approach. Though the list was long (about 800 names and out-of-date addresses on 18 pages), many people looked it over closely and made inquiries in their neighborhoods, churches, bridge clubs, etc. Several dozen answers were received containing information on from 1 to 45 people. The clues ranged from complete addresses to rather vague statements such as "I think he's selling real estate in Dallas." Even the latter helped immensely in many cases.

While this was going on, we were also working with the addresses from the old student directories and grade transcripts. With a stack of transcripts, an assistant sat down at the telephone and began phoning anyone in the Twin Cities phone directory with the same last name in the hopes of locating some relative. This approach was fruitful, though time consuming. Often people said that they were not part of the family involved, but they steered us to another branch of the family. Again, clues were given ranging from complete addresses to very vague musings.

Next, the information service of the telephone company was utilized. The Twin Cities telephone system lists telephone numbers by address as well as by name. For example, for an old student address of 3100 Grand Avenue, the operator was asked for the telephone number of 3100 Grand Avenue. Dialing that number, we asked the person who answered if he knew anything about a family named "_____" who used to live there. Fairly often the ownership of the house could be traced back through one or two buyers and these were contacted further. Almost everyone knows from whom they bought their house and generally has some rough idea of where the prior owner is currently living.

The next source was high school reunion lists. All of these people had been out of high school for slightly over 25 years, and it is a rare high school class that does not have a 25-year reunion. Usually someone in the class takes it upon himself (or, more often, herself) to locate everyone for this reunion. These individuals were very helpful. They were contacted through the high schools and frequently were able to provide a recent roster of their class with current addresses, occupations, and other information.

The high school reunion chairmen would have been an excellent source to use earlier. By the time we stumbled on this assistance, we had already been working for several months, using the methods described earlier. The reunion list would have been a far more efficient source to tap immediately, along with the phone book and the University alumni office.

Next in this progression, a brief letter was sent to the old address of the individuals still not located although, in most cases, we knew the individual did not live there anymore.

Considering the situation, the Post Office was remarkably successful. About 50 percent of these letters were delivered to either the individual or his relatives. Perhaps this was not too surprising in the small rural Minnesota towns. A student coming from Blackduck, Minnesota, has probably left many roots in the community, and it is not too hard to find him by mail, even a quarter of a century later. I have since been told that this approach might have been even more successful if the letters had been sent "certified mail with return receipt requested."

At this point, roughly 3 to 4 months later, 80 percent of the group had been located and the remainder were proving difficult to find. To maintain contact with the located 80 percent, each person was sent a 4-page mimeographed letter, which included a list of the 55 people still unlocated. People who had not taken the trouble to look through the first long list did scan this shorter one, and several more wanderers were located.

While all of this was going on, other miscellaneous methods were being used. Any student who had earned an advanced degree, e.g., an L.L.B, M.D., or Ph.D., was usually listed in the relevant professional directory, or perhaps was known to some member of the University faculty in that field. Also, the vital statistics file at the state capitol was searched for death certificates on any of the individuals or their parents who were still missing and this turned up a few names.

As is true in any large, applied research project, small "human interest" vignettes turned up all along the way. There was the "mother" who said, when asked of her son's whereabouts, "Oh, well, Richard wasn't like the rest of my children, he was adopted, you know, and he never seemed to get along with the rest of us. I haven't heard anything of him for 20 years." There was the girl named Anderson (which in Scandinavian Minnesota is like being named Jones) whom we couldn't find for several months. Finally, somehow, her married name turned up; it was reasonably distinctive and one day at lunch with a psychologist colleague of the same name, I asked him if he had ever heard of her. "Yes," he replied, "that's my wife."

After all sources had been exhausted, 21 names were left. At this point, a commercial locating agency, the Retail Credit Association, was contacted and asked to help. Their efficiency was chilling. Within 2 weeks (after we had spent 6 months), they supplied the current addresses of 16 of the 21 people, at an average cost of $18 per person. In discussions with them it became clear that their success was due to having historical information unavailable to most people—for example, a complete set of old Minneapolis phone books. In one case, they had followed a woman through the years by checking successive phone books until 1956 when she disappeared from the telephone book. They then checked wedding records for that year, found the woman had married and provided her married name and address, an address within a couple of miles of the University.

Another example of an individual who was difficult to locate might be illustrative. For one boy, very little information was available from 25 years ago. After the Retail Credit Association found him, this became understandable. In the 1930's his father was a Military Recruiting Officer assigned to Minneapolis for one year. The boy spent that one year at the University, just long enough to be in the Williamson-Bordin study, then moved on with his parents. Consequently, they had no neighborhood friends, he had no high school classmates in this area, and as he had not been involved in campus activities, none of his college classmates remembered him.

To add to this, the boy had followed his father in a service career and, as an adult, had been living the nomadic life demanded of career officers. Finding him was a tribute to the long arm of the Retail Credit Association.

At the end of 6 months, all but 5 of the original 768 had been located. Subsequently, in 2 or 3 cases, individuals with the right name turned out to be the wrong person and, in 3 or 4 others, although the individual was located once, he has since been lost. This last group consisted mostly of the homeless transients with "no permanent address." Thus, at a given time, about 98 to 99 percent of the group were located.

The individuals never located were mostly people without strong family ties. A few of them were listed in University records as orphans and wards of the court. In other cases, the parents were located and they said they had known nothing of their children for the past 10, 15 or 20 years, and they really didn't care.

SUMMARY OF THE LOCATING METHODS

This phase required about 6 months' work by the principal investigator, a half-time research assistant, and a half-time secretary. Though each did other work during this time, the major activity was this task of location. Though it is difficult to calculate, other costs probably totaled around $1000 for printing, postage, phone calls, and the Retail Credit Association bill.

From the experience of this project, several recommendations can be made for others with similar problems.

First, the telephone book and the Alumni Association are the best initial sources.

Second, the list sent to the located ones, asking for help in finding the missing ones, was a worthwhile method. Not only did it help find people, it gave the participants a feeling of involvement in the project.

Third, the letter to the old address should have been tried much earlier. An amazing number were delivered at a minimum cost.

Fourth, the high school reunion chairmen should have been contacted earlier. It was a fruitful source.

Fifth, the Retail Credit Association or some similar locating agency should have been used earlier.

In general, our recommendation is to get other individuals or offices working on the location problem, rather than trying to accomplish it with a research staff. The post office, reunion chairmen, and the Retail Credit Association were powerful allies.

WINNING COOPERATION

Once they were located, the next problem was to persuade these people to participate in this extensive survey.

The first contact with the group was made through a letter from the University President's office. It was a brief letter, stressing that the University of Minnesota has always been active in studying itself critically, emphasizing the importance of long-term research of this nature, and asking for their cooperation. In the same envelope went a letter from the project investigators, telling them specifically what was wanted, i.e., an interview, a questionnaire, and some tests.

The second contact was the list of the fellow students sent to them for their help in locating missing classmates. This gave them some involvement in the study and an unofficial side effect occurred. Through this list, they recognized friends who were also in this study. The topic apparently came up on many occasions, usually with a facilitating effect. One doctor verbalized this explicitly by saying, "All my friends are going to do it, so I suppose I should also."

After these initial contacts, time dragged as others were being located. To remind the located ones that we were still interested, a 4-page mimeographed letter was sent, telling them of progress made, relating some interesting (anonymous) anecdotes about their former classmates and trying to stimulate their curiosity and sense of humor. The stodgy, "researchish," academic approach was avoided, and the letter was informal and folksy.

All through these initial stages, the individuals were assured they would receive an extensive report of the results.

The next contact was made with individuals living within a 100-mile radius of the Twin Cities. During the spring of 1962, each of them was invited to a coffee hour on the University campus for the express purpose of taking the Minnesota Scholastic Aptitude Test (MSAT). At these coffee hours, one of the University's administrative personnel, usually a dean, spoke; the investigators reported on current progress; and again an attempt was made to make the participants feel committed to this project.

It was mainly a social time for them; coffee and doughnuts were served and they had a chance to talk to former classmates. Four coffee hours were held, netting a total of 125 MSATs and virtually assuring the participation of those individuals in the remaining phases of the study.

The same approach was used in Los Angeles, the other large concentration of former University students. Several coffee hours were held and, for those people willing to come to the UCLA campus, personal interviews were conducted at this time. Again, this proved helpful in winning the cooperation of the individuals involved.

The next contact was through the questionnaire mailed in June, 1962. The completed ones began coming in immediately, then the usual slump set in.

During the summer months a follow-up letter was mailed out, again attempting to stimulate curiosity by presenting a few tables based on the early returns. This touched off another wave of questionnaires, and they dribbled in throughout the remaining summer and fall months.

During the summer, each of these individuals was being contacted by an interviewer. Most of them were quite cooperative but, of course, there were a few reluctant ones, usually the same people who had not yet returned the questionnaire. However, while many people can ignore a questionnaire for weeks or even months, it is much harder to ignore a conscientious interviewer. We stressed to our interviewers that we wanted a very high percentage follow-up and asked them to be very persistent.

The interviewers in the Twin Cities area were graduate students from the University employed for this project as research assistants. For interviewers outside of Minnesota, resident psychologists were contacted and asked to do the interviewing or to recommend someone—usually a graduate student—who could do this. The interviewers were paid $10 plus travel expenses for each interview.

Interviewers were located for each individual, even those scattered throughout the world. A University staff member on leave in the Far East was able to do one in Hong Kong, a graduate student touring Europe picked up two in London, two in Paris, and one in Madrid. For a few foreign countries where no contact was readily available, correspondence directly with the American ambassador was successful in locating qualified people to do the interviewing. For one individual living far back in the Alaskan brush, it was impossible to find an interviewer. He was simply sent the interview booklet and asked to write in his own replies.

With a few exceptions, experiences with the interviewers were very good. The one change that might be recommended would be a higher fee for the interviewers. Ten dollars was barely adequate for arranging, traveling to, conducting, and reporting a 2-hour interview.

At the end of the interview schedule was a question, "Have you returned the questionnaire yet?" This proved to be a very powerful follow-up technique. The progress of the interviews in various cities could almost be charted by the number of questionnaires received.

During the school year, 1962–63, numerous attempts were made to follow up the non-respondents, whenever possible using the personal approach. Dozens of personal letters were sent; Dean E. G. Williamson wrote each person; long-distance telephone calls and telegrams were used when appropriate.

Some unexpected help came from a newspaper story published in the Minneapolis Sunday Star Tribune. It was a lengthy feature story on the study and was useful in persuading some of the holdouts that the study had merit.

Totally, the data collection phase stretched over a 12-month period, and achieved the results reported earlier in Table 14.

THE NON-RESPONDENTS

Some comment might be made about the 10 percent who refused to participate in this study. These non-respondents were compared with the respondents on a substantial number of variables, using data from the earlier Williamson-Bordin study. The most significant finding was that there were no major differences. On aptitude and achievement measures, the non-respondents averaged slightly lower than the others, but the differences were small.

There were bigger differences between the respondents and the 1 percent not located and the 4 percent deceased.

Table 15 presents the ability and achievement data at the time of college entrance for the group that took the MSAT and the three sub-groups that did not. The most deviant group was the deceased, a selection bias out of the hands of the investigator.

TABLE 15. *MSAT Takers versus Non-takers*

Groups	N	HSR Percentile		CAT Percentile		GPA*	
		M	S.D.	M	S.D.	M	S.D.
MSAT takers	634	74	22.3	63	24.9	2.17	.74
Refusals	97	72	24.1	58	26.0	2.12	.68
Unlocated	7	57	19.4	74	25.5	1.87	.67
Deceased	30	56	29.0	60	26.9	1.79	.79

*Based on undergraduate record (A = 4.0).

The many other comparisons made between the respondents and non-respondents showed even smaller differences. Because of that, and because the non-respondents were only a small portion of the total sample, the results are not reported here. While there was some slight trend for the respondents to be more successful, there was much overlapping. Some very successful individuals chose not to participate, while some abject failures were included in the respondent group. The most reasonable conclusion is that, while the non-respondents were certainly not a random sample, they were not grossly atypical.

I cannot refrain from reflecting here on the massive feelings of frustration generated by these non-respondents. After a year of intensive wheedling, cajoling and persuasion, the existence of a body of non-participants works a powerful Zeigarnik effect on an investigator. Near the end of the project, when these feelings of frustration were highest, one of the interviewers reported that one of her subjects, the chairman of an engineering department in a state university, just would not take the time to talk with her. In an unfortunate display of bad judgment and poor taste, I wrote to him:

> Dear Professor _____:
>   I have a letter from our interviewer there saying you have refused to cooperate with our study because it is "ridiculously long and time-consuming." On the slim chance that you are an academician who has an open mind toward other people's research, I thought I would write and tell you more about the project and, hopefully, persuade you to change your mind.
>   I start pessimistically, of course. You're probably aware of the research showing the rigidity of mental processes after about age twenty-five. Once a forty-five-year-old makes up his mind, apparently nothing—facts, emotions, pleas, etc.—will change it. However this solidification seems to proceed more slowly in bright people, and I'm pinning my hopes on your being bright enough to retain some flexibility. . . .
>   One finding that I was not prepared for is the resistance of college faculties toward this type of research. Although there are only a dozen or so Ph.D.s in this project, they constitute a significant portion of the uncooperative people. I guess this substantiates the research showing that research people tend to be asocial, introvertish, and insensitive to the feelings of others. Perhaps this is one reason that students frequently find the University a cold, impersonal place. . . .

Writing this letter gave me considerable cathartic relief, and it would have served its purpose well—had I just not mailed it. Needless to say, it did not endear me to him, he did not participate, and I probably have a life-long antagonist.

Perhaps it was worth it.

There were a variety of reasons that people would not participate, the most common one being their own illness, or illness of a close family member. It is hard to be very persistent in attempting to interview a man who is in bed recovering from a heart attack.

Usually, however, failures to accomplish interviews were due to irresponsible interviewers who kept maintaining they would do it "next week," but then procrastinated to the point where we had to eliminate the subject. The interviewers required persistent supervision.

One anecdote will demonstrate one of the unique reasons for lack of cooperation. One woman refused to have anything to do with us and it was only after considerable pumping in a long-distance phone call that she even agreed to tell me why.

"I'll never trust you researchers again," she said. "When I was at the University, a boy who worked in the Dean's office said to me, 'I just looked in your folder and I don't understand how you get such good grades—you didn't do so hot on the entrance test!' "

She went on to say, "It happened in a group of other students and I'll remember that embarrassment the rest of my life. Don't ever ask me to tell you anything else."

There is a lesson there for those responsible for the confidentialness of student records. The effects of leaks of information last 25 years.

CHAPTER SEVEN

HAPPINESS AND SATISFACTION

One presumed outcome of counseling is to help students to find careers in which they will be happy and satisfied. More generally, counseling should help the student to make full use of his resources, leading to more success and satisfaction in all areas of life. To determine if this occurred, it was necessary to find some way to measure these individuals on variables dealing with satisfaction and achievement. This chapter reports the attempt to assess the happiness and satisfaction of the counseled students as opposed to that of the non-counseled; Chapter 8 will report on their achievements.

Of course, any discussion about happiness, particularly its measurement, is fraught with philosophical perils. Is happiness an objective state of the environment or a subjective state of mind? Is it a unitary dimension or is it a composite of several other factors, such as marital happiness, job satisfaction, and healthy self-esteem? Is it, perhaps, a personality trait, such as aggressiveness, for example, so that there may be individuals who are happy no matter what the circumstances and others who are continually gloomy? A more basic question for counseling perhaps is: Should people be completely happy and satisfied, or would this foster too much apathy and acceptance of the status quo?

For the most part, this research has not come to grips with these questions. Instead, it has proceeded under three main assumptions. First, it's good for people to be happy—particularly to like their jobs. Second, people understand what is meant by the question, "Are you happy?" Third, their answers to such questions reflect accurately their true feelings. After making these assumptions, we have simply asked questions about happiness and satisfaction in a variety of ways, then have compared the groups on their answers.

Several measures of satisfaction were attempted:

1. Job satisfaction
2. Occupational satisfaction
3. Marital satisfaction
4. Satisfaction with social life
5. General satisfaction
6. Satisfaction with self

Many of these were crude measures, sometimes just one question on the interview. The first two, job and occupational satisfaction, were more crucial to the study and more elaborate scales were used. If counseling does indeed help students to find areas for which they are best fitted, this should show up first in the man's satisfaction with his occupation. Presumably, this will spill over into other areas of his life, for if he is happy in his work, he will probably be happier in other aspects such as marriage, social life, and general over-all feelings.

JOB SATISFACTION

The measure of job satisfaction used was the Hoppock Job Satisfaction Scale. Because we were more interested in the individual's satisfaction with his occupation rather than his specific job, a modification of the Job Satisfaction Scale was developed to use in measuring occupational satisfaction. The changes were slight, essentially substitution of the word, "occupation" for "job" in the items, and rewriting of the directions to give two separate sets for

TABLE 16. *Counseled versus Non-counseled on Occupation and Job Satisfaction Scales*

	N	Occupational Satisfaction M	Occupational Satisfaction S.D.	Job Satisfaction M	Job Satisfaction S.D.	Total Satisfaction M	Total Satisfaction S.D.
				Men			
Counseled	165	30.7	5.8	29.3	6.3	60.0	11.5
Non-counseled	106	31.3	6.6	30.2	7.2	61.1	13.1
		n.s.		n.s.		n.s.	
				Women*			
Counseled	105	27.7	7.7	25.9	8.0	53.5	15.0
Non-counseled	89	29.3	6.2	28.8	6.4	58.3	11.3
		n.s.		p<.01		p<.02	

*Included results of (1) current job; (2) if unemployed, past job.

answering the items, the first being, "Now think about your specific job" and the second, "Now forget about your job and think about your over-all occupation." A pilot study by White (1962) demonstrated that groups satisfied with their occupation but not their job could be separated from groups satisfied with both and satisfied with neither, by using the appropriate comparisons.

For the current study, the results from both scales and the composite are shown in Table 16 for both the counseled and non-counseled group.

Among the males, the evidence indicates that neither group was higher on these measures. This finding can be explained partially by the reassuring note that hardly any of them disliked their jobs. Table 17 shows the distribution of answers to one question from the Job Satisfaction Scale: "How do you like your job?" Only a few reported even indifference, and almost none reported extreme distaste. By age 45, apparently most people have found an occupation they are happy in, with or without counseling.

TABLE 17. *Answers to "How do you like your job?" for Counseled and Non-counseled Groups*

	Men		Women		Total	
	Counseled Percent	Non-counseled Percent	Counseled Percent	Non-counseled Percent	Counseled Percent	Non-counseled Percent
I hate it	0	1	0	0	0	1
I dislike it	2	0	6	0	3	0
I don't like it	6	5	7	1	7	4
I am indifferent to it	3	2	6	4	4	3
I like it	42	47	41	50	42	48
I am enthusiastic about it	38	36	36	37	38	36
I couldn't be more satisfied	9	10	4	6	7	8
N =	173	124	107	69	280	193

However, among the women, the non-counseled group was significantly higher on two of the three satisfaction measures reported in Table 16, and on the composite scale, the difference was roughly one-third standard deviation, a difference large enough to be practically meaningful. The conclusion must be that counseled women were less satisfied vocationally.

Possibly this was because the counseled women were more career oriented and less satisfied with the domestic role. Comparing the two groups on the scales of the SVIB showed that the counseled women were significantly higher on the following scales:

Psychologist	(.01 level)
Social worker	(.10)
Lawyer	(.10)
Social science teacher	(.10)
YWCA secretary	(.10)
Physical education teacher	(.10)

and significantly lower than the non-counseled women on these scales:

Musician-teacher	(.01)
M-F	(.05)
Musician-performer	(.05)
Buyer	(.05)
Housewife	(.10)
Elementary teacher	(.10)
Office worker	(.10)
Steno-secretary	(.10)
Business education teacher	(.10)

Thus, there was a tendency for the counseled women to be less domestic and more intellectual in their interests than the non-counseled. The cluster of scales usually interpreted as "pre-marital" (housewife, elementary teacher, office worker, and steno-secretary) favored the non-counseled while the intellectual-verbal scales (psychologist, lawyer, social worker) favored the non-counseled. The same small trend was apparent in the positions actually held, since 34 percent of the non-counseled women had been homemakers exclusively since leaving college compared with 27 percent of the counseled.

It may be that the women employed outside the home are mildly less satisfied with their jobs and, because more of them were counseled, this could explain the difference on the satisfaction scales. (Unfortunately, this assertion could not be tested directly as we neglected to ask the women which job they had in mind when they were filling in the questionnaire. Some of them apparently answered in regard to their last job outside the home, while others answered in regard to their current position as homemaker.)

Because there were no differences found in favor of the counseled group in the vocational realm, it may not be reasonable to expect them to rate higher than the non-counseled group in other areas of satisfaction. Most counseling, certainly that done at Minnesota in the 1930's, directs its attention to the vocational aspect of the student's choices, and if no difference can be detected in these outcomes, there is little chance that measures of marital satisfaction, social satisfaction, or general satisfaction will show any results either.

Consequently, it should be no surprise that the groups were virtually identical on these measures also. Again, the reason may be that most of these people were happy and content with their situations.

MARITAL SATISFACTION

Two gross measures of marital satisfaction were used. The first was the individual's self-report elicited during the interview. The interviewer asked the subject to describe some of the good things about his marriage, then some of the bad things, then asked him to rate his marriage in terms of general satisfaction. The specific question asked and the percent responding to each category are reported in Table 18.

TABLE 18.   *Self-ratings and Interviewer Ratings of Marital Satisfaction*

"Taking all things together, how would you describe your marriage, as very satisfying, about average, or not as satisfying as it should have been?"*

Self-rating (in Percentages)

	Men		Women		Total	
	Counseled	Non-counseled	Counseled	Non-counseled	Counseled	Non-counseled
Very satisfying	71	73	67	69	68	70
Fairly satisfying	10	12	8	8	9	10
Average	11	14	17	13	14	13
Fairly dis-satisfying	4	0	2	3	3	1
Very dis-satisfying	3	2	6	9	5	5
N =	178	130	174	118	352	248

Interviewer Rating (in Percentages)

	Men		Women		Total	
	Counseled	Non-counseled	Counseled	Non-counseled	Counseled	Non-counseled
Happy	43	42	41	38	42	40
Pleased	27	26	28	29	27	28
Satisfied	19	21	19	17	19	19
Resigned	7	9	5	9	6	9
Unhappy	4	2	7	7	6	5
N =	177	127	166	113	343	240

*Though the individual was given only three categories, the interviewers were asked to assign the answer to one of the five categories listed.

Also reported in that table are the ratings made by the interviewer of the person's marital satisfaction. This rating, made after the interview was completed, was based on the interviewer's total impression of the person's marriage.

Clearly, there was no difference between the counseled and non-counseled students on this variable. The only trend appearing in the data is that, though the scales are not completely comparable, the individual's rating of his marriage was higher, on the average, than the interviewer's rating of that same marriage.

SATISFACTION WITH SOCIAL LIFE

In the interview the question was asked, "Do you have as many social contacts as you would like, or would you rather have more or less?" the results are shown in Table 19.

TABLE 19. *Satisfaction with Social Life*

	Men		Women		
	Counseled Percent	Non-counseled Percent	Counseled Percent	Non-counseled Percent	Total Percent
Would like more contacts	31	30	34	21	30
Have enough contacts	60	66	58	68	61
Would like fewer contacts	8	4	9	11	8
N =	191	135	197	131	654

The trend appeared very similar to that found on the occupational satisfaction measures. There were no differences between the men, but the counseled women appeared less happy with their social life though, again, the majority of both sexes were comfortable with the current situation.

The next question was, "If you could, in what ways would you change your social life?" The answers to that question, categorized in Table 20, give some indication of the types of social unhappiness felt by these people.

The major change these people would want is more social contact with others, and the counseled group mentioned it significantly more often than the non-counseled. Further, the non-counseled mentioned "None" significantly more often than the counseled. Though the differences are small, only 7 to 8 points, they consistently indicate that the counseled individuals were less happy with

TABLE 20. *Desired Changes in Social Life*

	Men		Women		Total	
	Counseled	Non-counseled	Counseled	Non-counseled	Counseled	Non-counseled
None	38	49	27	32	33	40
Fewer required business contacts	9	7	8	7	9	7
Have more friends, entertain more	27	21	38	29	33	25
Have more intimate friends	4	2	4	5	4	4
Attend more formal and cultural events	9	10	6	12	7	11
More time with family	3	1	5	4	4	3
Fewer social contacts	1	2	2	1	2	2
Have more money	1	1	2	3	2	2
More travel and outdoor activities	4	2	2	3	3	2
Other	3	5	5	5	4	5
N =	213	145	226	151	439	296

their situations. This trend, always small, will be frequently re-
peated in the following pages.

GENERAL SATISFACTION AND ADJUSTMENT

Several different indexes of general satisfaction were tried.
First, each individual was asked to compare himself with others
in terms of his satisfaction with life. Second, each person was asked
to judge his own happiness and satisfaction against a more absolute measure. Third, each person was rated by the interviewer on
a general adjustment scale.

For the first method the person was asked "When you left the
University life, would you say you were as satisfied with the way
things were going for you as the average college student, or were
you more or less satisfied?"

The same question, appropriately modified, was asked about
their current satisfaction, and also for what they predicted their
lives would be 5 to 10 years from now. There were no differences
between the counseled and non-counseled groups. The data were
interesting, however, as they did show differences over the various
time periods. As Table 21 shows, there was a strong trend for
people to feel more satisfied now than they remembered being
25 years ago.

TABLE 21. *Satisfaction Compared with Others (Percentages)*

	Immediately after Leaving University	Now	5-10 years from now
More satisfied than others	23	54	56
Same	44	38	39
Less satisfied	33	7	5
N =	654	649	633

There was one mild difference between sexes that does not show in this table. More of the men than the women (62 versus 47 percent) felt that their life 5 to 10 years in the future would be better. From comments made in the interviews, this seems partially due to uncertainty among the women about what they would do with themselves after their children were grown. Many of the women could see that 5 to 10 years later all of their children would have left the home; this caused them some concern about what their life would be like at that time.

One other substantial difference appeared in the tabulations. Substantially more non-graduates than graduates (53 to 22 percent) reported themselves less satisfied than the average student when they left the University. That was not surprising; graduates should feel more satisfaction. What was surprising was the lack of any current difference between these two groups. Non-graduates today reported as much satisfaction as graduates, and were even slightly more optimistic about the future (58 percent to 52 percent, respectively), expecting life to be better in the future.

The second method of assessing the individual's over-all satisfaction used a method suggested by Kilpatrick and Cantril (1960). It requires the individual to judge his situation against what he feels is an ideal situation. This method recognizes that a person's happiness is dependent on what he expects from life and asks him to decide just how far he is from what he considers to be the best possible situation.

Each person was asked, "Imagine a ladder with 10 rungs. The top rung, No. 10, represents the ideal life and the bottom rung, No. 1, represents the worst possible life. On what rung do you think you are?" The question was asked for three periods in their life: first, when they left the University; second, now; and third, 5 years from now.

Again, there was essentially no difference between the answers of the counseled and non-counseled groups, or between sexes, but there were great differences over the various time periods. Table 22 shows three distributions, labeled according to the time periods they represent.

TABLE 22.   *Distribution of Self-reports on "Ladder of Success" Scale*

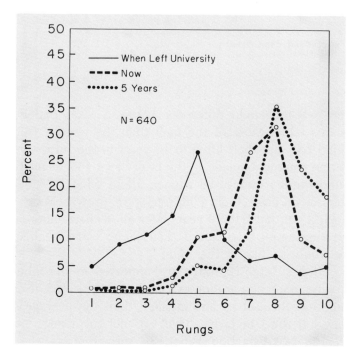

The dominant theme demonstrated by this chart was the high level of satisfaction indicated by most people. About 7 percent of them put themselves on rung 10, 50 percent on rung 8 or above, and 75 percent on rung 7 or above. At least on this criterion, the large majority of people were satisfied with their current life. As most of them liked their jobs, were making good salaries, were healthy, and comfortable in marriage, this was a reasonable finding.

(There were a few quixotic cases. One man who put himself

TABLE 23.   *Interviewer's Rating of General Adjustment (in Percentages)*

	Men		Women		Total	
	Counseled	Non-counseled	Counseled	Non-counseled	Counseled	Non-counseled
Very unhappy	3	1	6	2	4	2
Resigned	10	9	13	13	11	11
Satisfied	20	28	22	24	21	26
Pleased	41	35	34	31	38	33
Very happy	26	27	24	30	25	28
N =	190	134	197	131	387	265

on rung 10 was obviously having a great deal of marital strife, had a job that he didn't particularly care for, and children who were having some adjustment problems. His explanation: "I spend my spare time bringing the word of God to others and that is the best possible life.")

The third measure of personal happiness, again a gross measure, was the interviewer's rating of adjustment. The five rating categories and percent assigned to each are reported in Table 23.

Hardly any trend can be teased out of this table except that the large majority of both groups were, in the eyes of the interviewers, satisfied with their situation.

THE INDIVIDUAL'S SATISFACTION WITH HIMSELF

The individual's satisfaction with himself was tapped in a question that read, "Many people would like their children to be different from themselves. How would you like your son/daughter to be different from you?"

The answers are arranged in Table 24 so that those mentioned more often by the counseled people are at the top of the table. They mentioned more ways they would like their children to be different and there was a clear theme running through the comments. The counseled parents want their children to have more self-confidence, be more mature, less anxious, and not so shy. The non-counseled want their children to have a better education, a happier childhood, more intelligence and a different occupation. The two groups chose different, though overlapping, frameworks to describe

TABLE 24. *Percent Responses to the Question: "How would you like your child to be different from you?"*

	Counseled	Non-counseled	Difference
Have more self-confidence	9	4	5
Be more mature — more of a goal in mind	8	3	5
Be less anxious — not take things so seriously	8	5	3
Be more adequate in interpersonal relations — less shy	27	24	3
Some physical change — taller, prettier, etc.	8	7	1
Be less of an extrovert	2	1	1
Have more money or security	3	2	1
Just be better in every way	4	3	1
Be less compulsive	1	0	1
Be the same as I am	27	27	0
Have more outside interests	3	3	0
Be more compulsive	2	2	0
Have a different occupation	2	3	-1
Be more aggressive — have more drive	11	13	-2
Be brighter — have more intelligence	5	7	-2
Have a happier childhood	3	5	-2
Have better education	6	10	-4

their weaknesses. The counseled students were more introspective, more apt to locate the source of inadequacies in themselves, while the non-counseled group cited outside influences.

This table suggests a theme that will be developed in greater detail in the next several paragraphs. It is that these counseled adults, like the current college students seeking counseling, were more anxious and tense than the non-counseled group.

For example, to the question "Are you a worrier?" 61 percent of the non-counseled versus 48 percent of the counseled said, "No," a substantial and significant difference.

Further, this theme was apparent in the answers given to a medical check list included in the questionnaire. The main purpose of this check list was to insert items usually associated with emotional discomfort, such as "ulcers" or "nervousness." The list and the percentages replying affirmatively to each category are listed

TABLE 25. *Health Problems Reported by Counseled and Non-counseled Students*

	Counseled Percent	Non-counseled Percent
Reported more often by counseled		
"Other"	12	8
Asthma or hay fever	10	5
Nervousness	5	3
Ulcers	5	2
High blood pressure	4	3
No difference between groups		
Physical disability	10	10
Heart trouble	2	2
Emotional disorder	1	1
Cancer	1	1
Diabetes	1	1
None	59	72

in Table 25. Those items reported more often by the counseled are listed first; the items reported equally by each group are listed next, there were no items reported more often by the non-counseled group.

All the ailments reported more often by the counseled, with the possible exception of "other," are commonly supposed to be more psychosomatic in nature than most of those reported equally by both groups. The differences are small, but their consistency is remarkable.

This theme of introspective anxiety ran through another set of questions, those concerning sources of help for personal problems. The next section reports the answers to a series of questions on that point.

SEEKING PROFESSIONAL HELP AS ADULTS

Do counseled students, as adults, utilize professional sources for solving personal problems more often than non-counseled students? If so, is this because they have more personal problems or is it because they more often appreciate the value of these services?

TABLE 26. *Sources of Professional Help*

"Have you ever gone to a professional person for advice and help with any personal problem?"	Counseled		Non-counseled	
	N	Percent	N	Percent
<u>NO</u>	255	66	204	78
If NO: Do you think you would ever have a personal problem that got so bad you might want to go someplace for help, or do you think you would always handle things like that by yourself?				
Seek help		48		37
Handle by self		47		57
No response		6		5
<u>YES</u>	132	34	61	22
If YES: What was the reason for seeking help?				
<u>More often given by counseled</u>				
My own emotional problem		39		21
<u>Given about equally</u>				
Emotional or scholastic problem with child		24		25
Emotional problem of spouse		5		5
Alcoholism of myself or spouse		2		2
Other		11		12
<u>More often given by non-counseled</u>				
Emotional problems of other family members		2		4
My own physical problem		2		5
Physical problem with child		3		7
Religious problem		2		7
Marriage problem		15		26

The answer to the first question, based on data from this study was "Yes, counseled students, as adults, do use professional services more often." They utilize different types of professional people and report different types of problems from the non-counseled. Relevant information on these points was collected in both the questionnaire and the interview and is reported in the next few pages.

The second question posed above (Is this because the counseled students have more personal problems or because they have more appreciation for the value of these services?) was more difficult to answer and while the following discussion reports some pertinent information, the question remained essentially unanswered.

In the questionnaire to be filled out by the participants was the question, "Have you ever gone to a psychiatrist or a psychologist?" Twice as many of the counseled students as non-counseled students said "Yes," 20 to 10 percent. In the later interview the same question was asked in a slightly different manner, and the analogous percentages were 19 to 10 percent. (There was not complete overlap between the two samples.)

In the interview a series of questions was asked on this point. They are listed in Table 26 with the responses given by both groups.

There are some intriguing differences in these answers. Not only do more of the non-counseled students say they have never sought help (78 to 66 percent) but substantially more of them say that they cannot visualize a personal problem so bad that they ever would (57 to 47 percent).

A similar theme runs through the second half of the table where the reasons for seeking help are reported. The counseled students more often reported the problem was their own emotional one (39 to 21 percent) while, without exception, the differences in favor of the non-counseled students were those in which the problem was attributed to someone else, i.e., child, or spouse, or marriage. The non-counseled students simply did not report so many personal problems.

Was this because they had fewer problems, or was it because they refused to recognize them? It was impossible to establish a clear answer to that question from the available information, but it seemed likely that both explanations had some relevance. While there were only the mildest of differences reported on the satisfaction measures, they were in favor of the non-counseled group. Earlier it was shown the students who seek counseling are slightly more uncomfortable than those who do not; perhaps this difference was being demonstrated once again.

The alternative explanation—that counseled students might be more willing to recognize the existence of a problem—also seems very likely as there was a consistent theme running throughout these answers, i.e., the non-counseled students seemed less willing to verbalize the existence of, or the eventual possibility of, a serious personal problem. Even in the sources of help they reported using, the non-counseled students were less likely to accept the possibility of an emotional problem. In Table 27 those reported sources are listed, separated into two clusters, according to whether the counseled or non-counseled group reported the more contact.

TABLE 27. *Reported Source of Professional Help by Counseled and Non-counseled Students*

	Counseled Percent	Non-counseled Percent
Sought more often by counseled		
Psychiatrist	38	30
Psychologist	19	13
Marriage counselor	15	10
Child guidance clinic	6	2
Sought more often by non-counseled		
Minister	17	28
Doctor	12	26
Social worker	5	8
Lawyer	5	7
Friend	1	2
Other	3	10
	*	*
N =	130	61

* Percentages add to more than 100 because of multiple answers.

The two clusters are distinct and meaningful; those used by the counseled people are professional persons more highly trained to deal with problems of emotional distress and are probably viewed by the general public as almost exclusively involved with those types of problems. Those used by the non-counseled represent different kinds of professional persons; usually, they are neither by training nor personal inclination equipped to handle intense personal emotional problems, and there are more socially acceptable reasons for consulting with these men than with those in the first cluster.

To the question, Do non-counseled students, as adults, have fewer personal problems, or do they simply refuse to recognize them? the second alternative seems the more reasonable choice. The former non-counseled students have not sought help so often, and less often say they will in the future, no matter what happens. When they have sought help, they more often reported that they did it for someone else, and they shied away from sources of professional help usually associated with emotional problems.

It appears that the counseled students were more willing to deal openly with these types of problems.

Can an hour or two in a counselor's office 25 years ago really have created this difference?

SUMMARY

Results presented in this chapter indicate that there were only small differences between the counseled and non-counseled groups on the measures of satisfaction but, where those differences did appear, they consistently showed the counseled individuals to be slightly more discontented with life.

Evidence from a variety of measures indicated that the counseled individuals were more anxious in an introspective sort of way. They worried more, they admitted to more emotional problems, they more often have sought professional help, they say they want their children to have more self-confidence than they themselves had, they voiced more psychosomatic complaints, and they scored lower on an occupational satisfaction scale.

It is not clear whether these differences were created by the counseling 25 years ago. Earlier it was shown that students seeking counseling report more personal discomfort than those who do not, and this behavior may persist into adulthood. Whatever its source, this discovery of a thread of discontentment running through the counseled group is a fascinating one worthy of further study.

CHAPTER EIGHT

ACHIEVEMENT

Do counseled students ultimately achieve any more than non-counseled students? This chapter explores the general area of success and achievement, using three different types of measures: first, academic success; second, objective listings of publications, patents, elected offices, income, etc.; and third, a subjective rating of achievement.

ACADEMIC ACHIEVEMENT

This section is concerned with the academic accomplishments of the students, such as graduation rates, grade point average (GPA), and campus participation, while they were at the University of Minnesota.

ACADEMIC APTITUDE

Before discussing these results, it is necessary to compare the groups on two measures that are known to be related to academic achievement, High School Rank (HSR) and College Aptitude Test (CAT) score. In the original Williamson-Bordin study, the groups were matched on these variables and this matching has been maintained in some of the comparisons in this report. In other comparisons, the total counseled group has been compared with the total non-counseled group; however, those of the original non-counseled group who later came in for counseling have been moved into the counseled group, disturbing the original matching.

To indicate the effect of the disturbance, the means and standard deviations for the groups, separated by sex, are reported in Table 28.

None of the differences was statistically significant, and all of them were small. Thus, these variables can be ignored in the subsequent discussions.

TABLE 28. *Comparison between Counseled and Non-counseled Follow-up Cases on Academic Aptitude Measures at Time of Entrance to the University*

	Males				Females			
	Counseled		Non-counseled		Counseled		Non-counseled	
	Mean	S.D.	Mean	S.D.	Mean	S.D.	Mean	S.D.
High School Rank	67	24	69	24	79	20	79	19
College Aptitude Test Percentile	64	26	62	25	63	25	61	25
N =	238		159		214		155	

GRADE POINT AVERAGE

As reported earlier in the Williamson-Bordin study, the average first quarter GPA for the counseled students was 2.18, for the non-counseled student 1.97. The final over-all grade point was 2.20 for the counseled and 2.06 for the non-counseled. Both of these differences were statistically significant ($p < .01$), and both of them were large enough to have some practical import. If counseling did nothing more than raise the students' GPA by two-tenths of a point (about a third of a standard deviation), it would be worthwhile.

DEGREES EARNED

Next, using information from official University transcripts, the two groups were compared on number of degrees earned. That information is given in Table 29.

These data illustrate a healthy difference between the two groups in graduation frequency. Fifty-nine percent of the counseled group received some 4-year degree compared to 48 percent of the non-counseled group. This difference was statistically significant and has obvious practical significance. Any student personnel program that can increase the graduation rate by one-fourth (the rise from 48 to 59 percent) is clearly of value to the over-all educational mission of the University.

It was possible that this difference might disappear if the two groups were compared using *all* of the degrees earned, whether at

TABLE 29.   *Highest Degree Earned at University of Minnesota by Counseled and Non-counseled Students*

	Counseled Group		Non-counseled Group		Total	
	N	Percent	N	Percent	N	Percent
None	186	41	164	52	350	46
A.L.A. (2-year degree)	9	2	2	1	11	1
B.A.	197	44	111	35	308	40
M.A.	26	6	8	2	34	4
D.D.S.	4	1	4	1	8	1
L.L.B.	10	2	8	2	18	2
M.D.	12	3	16	5	28	4
Ph.D.	9	2	1	-	10	1
Number of individuals with B.A. or higher	266	59	148	48	414	54
Total N	453		314		767*	

*Transcript unavailable for one individual.

Minnesota or elsewhere. Perhaps counseling simply kept students in school at Minnesota while the non-counseled students moved to other institutions. That possibility was tested by using the data reported by the individuals in the questionnaires. Among the non-graduate group, 13 percent of the counseled versus 9 percent of the non-counseled earned B.A.s elsewhere and, among the total group, graduate degrees were earned elsewhere by 8 percent of the counseled versus 4 percent of the non-counseled. Thus, even at institutions other than Minnesota, counseled students graduated more frequently.

A second group was studied in much the same manner and provided a replication of Table 29. This was the random sample discussed earlier on page 26, selected with the same composition of sex and year of entry as the Williamson-Bordin sample. The degrees earned by the counseled and non-counseled students in that sample are shown in the next table.

This table shows the same difference in favor of the counseled group. The percentage earning "no degree" was higher in this sample because in the Williamson-Bordin sample, the counseled students were drawn from those who stayed in school at least one-quarter and the control students were drawn from those who stayed

TABLE 30. *Degrees Earned at Minnesota by Random Sample of
1933 to 1936 Freshmen Separated into Counseled and
Non-counseled Groups*

	Counseled		Non-counseled		Total	
	Number	Percent	Number	Percent	Number	Percent
No degree	155	50	304	63	459	58
A.L.A.	13	4	8	2	21	3
B.A.	115	37	127	26	242	31
M.A.	12	4	13	3	25	3
D.D.S.	3	1	5	1	8	1
L.L.B.	2	1	5	1	7	1
M.D.	4	1	16	3	20	2
Ph.D.	4	1	4	1	8	1

at least one year, a selection bias which would slightly increase the
graduation rate. (This bias, incidentally, would favor the non-
counseled group.)

Taken together, these two samples demonstrate conclusively
that a greater percentage, roughly 12 percent, of counseled students graduated than non-counseled students; that is, the graduation rate among counseled students was one-fourth higher than
among non-counseled students.

COUNSELING AND GRADUATE DEGREES

One further trend should be noted in these figures. The differences between the two groups were most prominent among the
B.A., M.A., and Ph.D. categories, the academic degrees, as opposed
to the professional degrees of D.D.S., L.L.B., and M.D. This was
probably because students planning professional careers as den-
tists, lawyers, and doctors were less apt to seek vocational counseling. These are familiar occupations, and frequently the decision
to enter one of them is made relatively early, many times as a
result of a strong family tradition.

On the other hand, occupations requiring an M.A. or Ph.D.
are not so familiar and students contemplating them might have
sought out special advice. Perhaps the initial idea of such a profession was planted by the counselor; especially with a bright
student, a counselor might be the first to suggest the possibility
of graduate school.

That this latter possibility is a likely one is demonstrated in
the Tables 31 and 32, which show the averages on several aptitude
measures of the various degree earners, separated into counseled
and non-counseled groups.

Although the numbers were usually too small for the differences to be significant, with one exception (HSR among the M.A.

TABLE 31. *Aptitude Measures for Degree Earners in Counseled and Non-counseled Groups (Williamson-Bordin Sample)*

	Percentile College Aptitude Test				Percentile High School Rank				Undergraduate GPA			
	Counseled		Non-counseled		Counseled		Non-counseled		Counseled		Non-counseled	
	N	Mean	N	Mean	N	Mean	N	Mean	N	Mean	N	Mean
None	155	59	139	57	154	61	139	67	155	1.7	139	1.6
B.A.	198	63	126	66	198	78	126	79	198	2.4	126	2.4
D.D.S.	4	42	4	32	4	65	4	68	4	2.3	4	2.5
L.L.B.	18	75	10	57	18	82	10	77	18	2.5	10	2.6
M.A.	41	69	12	64	41	77	12	83	41	2.6	12	2.4
M.D.	14	70	18	72	14	82	18	82	14	2.7	18	2.7
Ph.D.	23	79	5	66	23	78	5	63	23	2.9	5	2.8
	Random Sample of 1933 to 1936 Freshmen											
None	151	53	293	55	145	64	275	61				
B.A.	115	64	123	60	109	77	114	77				
D.D.S.	3	31	5	47	3	43	3	78				
L.L.B.	2	64	5	90	2	66	5	84				
M.A.	12	62	12	56	12	89	12	85				
M.D.	4	94	16	70	4	89	16	85				
Ph.D.	4	79	4	66	4	94	4	61				

winners), the counseled students earning M.A.s and Ph.D.s scored higher on all measures than the non-counseled. One of two explanations (or both) is possible: either counselors *encourage bright people* to continue their education beyond the B.A. or they *discourage mediocre ones* from attempting anything further. One does not have to be around a university counseling bureau long to see both situations.

This possibility that counselors may have considerable influence on the student's plans for graduate school is an intriguing one, and further relevant data were collected. If counselors do guide individuals into graduate work, this should show up in the

TABLE 32. *Percent of Ph.D.s and B.A.s Who Have Been Counseled*

	Science, Literature and Arts		Education		Institute of Technology		Agriculture		Total	
	N	Percent Counseled	N	Percent Counseled	N	Percent Counseled	N	Percent Counseled	N	Percent Counseled
B.A.	150	49	150	28	150	31	150	31	600	35
Ph.D.	250	58	87	47	96	40	110	36	543	49

percentage of counseled students earning different degrees. For example, a higher percentage of Ph.D.s should have been counseled than B.A.s.

To test this hypothesis, a random sample of 30 students was drawn from the graduation lists of each of the major undergraduate colleges at Minnesota for the even-numbered years from 1952 to 1960. For a sample of Ph.D.s, all individuals who earned that degree at Minnesota from 1952 to 1961, and who also were undergraduates at Minnesota, were used. The percent counseled in each group is presented in Table 32.

Within all colleges, the counseled percentage among Ph.D. earners was higher than among B.A. earners, usually by a substantial margin. Over-all, 49 per cent of the Ph.D.s were counseled versus 35 per cent of the B.A.s. The real difference may have been even larger as no attempt was made to screen the eventual Ph.D. winners from the B.A. group.

These data support the contention that counseling had some effect on the student's plans for graduate study, but they do not explain how this happened. Earlier (p. 32) it was shown that current high school seniors who are planning to go to graduate school are more apt to seek counseling than the average college student. Why do they come to the counselor, and how can they best be served? These questions need answering.

GRADUATION AND
FOLLOWING THE COUNSELOR'S ADVICE

In the earlier study, Williamson and Bordin rated each student, one year after counseling, on how closely the student followed

TABLE 33. *Final GPA and Graduation Rate by Different Levels of Agreement with Counseling Plan*

	\multicolumn{9}{c	}{Extent of Agreement}
	Close			Some			None		
	N	Mean	S.D.	N	Mean	S.D.	N	Mean	S.D.
Male									
Final GPA	129	2.36	.64	57	1.91	.73	11	1.73	.42
Percent receiving 4-year degree	78			60			36		
Female									
Final GPA	120	2.48	.68	56	1.88	.69	10	1.74	.76
Percent receiving 4-year degree	76			34			10		

the plans agreed upon by him and the counselor. It was a three-point rating, the first point signifying considerable agreement between the counseling plan and the student's subsequent course of action; the second point, some agreement; and the third, no agreement.

The average GPA and the percent graduating in each of those three categories is presented in Table 33.

The trend is unmistakably clear. Those students who most closely followed the counseling plan succeeded best.

ACADEMIC HONORS

Counseled students graduated more often so it was not surprising to find that they also won more academic honors than non-counseled students. Again the differences were not great but they inevitably favored the counseled student.

Two sources were used to collect information about honors. The first was the official University transcript which noted if the student had graduated Cum Laude, Magna Cum Laude, or Summa Cum Laude. That information is presented in Table 34.

TABLE 34. *Percentage of Counseled and Non-counseled Students Graduating with Honors*

	Counseled	Non-counseled
Cum Laude	6.0	5.7
Magna Cum Laude	2.9	1.6
Summa Cum Laude	1.1	0

TABLE 35. *Academic Awards and Honors Earned by Counseled and Non-counseled Students*

"Listed below are a number of awards and honors. Which of these did you receive during college?"	Counseled Percent	Non-counseled Percent
Dean's list (for high scholarship)	4	3
Phi Beta Kappa	6	2
Other honor society based on academic achievement	16	7
Graduation with honors (Cum, Magna, Summa)*	12	9
Honor society based on leadership	6	4
Other scholarship awarded on the basis of academic ability	4	1
Participation in "honors program" at this school	2	0
Prize or award for scholarship or research work	1	0
Prize or award for literary, musical, or artistic work	1	0
Took one or more graduate-level courses as an undergraduate	10	6
Other award or honor	6	5
None	65	75

*Including honors won at other universities.

The other source was the individual's questionnaire completed as part of the current study. Each was asked to check a list
of honors earned in college. The list and the percentage of each
group checking each category are presented in Table 35. Counseled students reported more earned honors in every category.

CAMPUS PARTICIPATION AND LEADERSHIP

We also asked each former student about his participation in
campus activities and whether he had held elected offices in those
activities. Tables 36 and 37 give those figures.

TABLE 36. *Percentage of Counseled and Non-counseled Students
Participating in Campus Activities*

"In which of the following were you an active participant during college?"	Counseled	Non-counseled
Editorial staff of campus publication	9	5
Musical or dramatic group	18	12
Business staff of campus publication or other campus group	4	2
Campus group concerned with national or world issues	9	6
Inter-collegiate (varsity) athletics	8	6
Fraternity, or equivalent	47	38
Special interest group(e.g., Psychology Club, Rover's Club)	16	10
Student government	10	4
YMCA, other religious groups	33	23
Off-campus organizations	23	24
None	14	26

TABLE 37. *Number of Elected Offices Held in College by
Counseled and Non-counseled Students*

Number	Counseled Percent	Non-counseled Percent
None	80	88
1	9	7
2	6	3
3	4	2
4	0	0
5	1	0

Counseled students were more active in a wide range of student activities including athletics, music, student government, and
religious organizations, and, more often than their non-counseled
peers, they were leaders in those activities. Not only were the
counseled students (slightly) better students but they were
(slightly) more involved in campus life in general.

To summarize thus far, it is clear the counseled students led
more fruitful collegiate lives than the non-counseled. They earned
better grades, higher honors, more degrees (with the exception of

the professional degrees), participated in more campus activities and more often held leadership positions in those activities.

CURRENT ACHIEVEMENTS

In this section will be presented the information on the current achievements of the individuals being studied. All of these data were gathered during 1961–62 when these people were roughly 45 years old.

The study of achievement beyond college days creates some problems. Life does not furnish official transcripts and adult activities are not strung out in credit hours with a Phi Beta Kappa key dangling at the end. Inevitably, any list of criteria selected will have some weaknesses. These inevitable disadvantages should not prevent all attempts to generate knowledge in this area and, to that end, two approaches were tried.

First, the individuals were asked to list specific honors and awards they had won. Second, all of these data, along with other available information on each person, were used to rate each person on his success in contributing to society.

The first approach attempted to measure achievement by asking the individual to list his honors or awards, such as patents, artistic prizes, invited addresses, publications, and the like. Although initially this approach may seem to be objective, it was, at best, a crude one. It used the individual's self-report, and people vary in what they consider to be an honor. Also, some people, because of their situation, have more opportunities to win awards than the average person. For example, even a mediocre research engineer is likely to have more patents than the average college graduate. But hopefully these situational restrictions were randomly distributed between the counseled and control groups.

Specific Honors and Awards Won

Table 38 lists the question as it was asked, and the frequency of each group replying positively for each category. The reported figure is the percentage of each group saying something other than "none."

There was a mild tendency for the counseled individuals to report more intellectual accomplishments while the non-counseled reported more military and business achievements. Probably these trends could be explained by the larger number of M.A. and Ph.D. degrees among the counseled group.

TABLE 38.   *Honors, Awards, and Achievements of Counseled and Non-counseled Students*

	Counseled Percent	Non-counseled Percent	Difference
Non-fiction articles and books published	8	3	+5
Other publications not indicated elsewhere	9	5	+4
Athletic awards	8	5	+3
Invitational address (i.e., Wm. James Lecture at Harvard)	4	2	+2
Patents	2	0	+2
Technical articles or books published	15	14	+1
Awards for music	1	0	+1
Fiction articles and books published	2	2	0
Awards for dramatic productions and performances	1	2	-1
Civic awards	9	10	-1
Armed Forces decorations awarded on individual basis	8	10	-2
Awards for art	0	2	-2
Professional or business awards	8	11	-3
* * *			
Has your spouse received anything of the above nature?	16	11	+5

Several other objective questions, which presumably measured achievement, were asked on the questionnaire. These questions were based on the rationale that if a person is successful, he will more often speak publicly and more often be elected to offices of one sort or another.

Three questions pertaining to these activities are listed in Table 39 with the percentage of each group that replied affirmatively.

TABLE 39.   *Public Appearances and Elected Offices of Counseled and Non-counseled Students*

Questions Asked	Percentage Replying "Yes"	
	Counseled	Non-counseled
Have you ever been on TV?	25	22
Have you given any speeches in the past 2 years?	47	42
Have you been elected to any offices in the past 2 years?	54	54

Again, there was only the mildest of trends in favor of the counseled group, so mild that the prudent investigator (and reader) should not call further attention to it.

INCOME AS A MEASURE OF ACHIEVEMENT

There are probably few counselors who would agree to having their effectiveness evaluated by the size of the student's income 25 years later. Certainly, there are many reasons why it is an imperfect measure for these purposes. The end product of counseling is not to make people wealthy, nor is that the ultimate aim of higher education. Even if earning power were accepted as a legitimate aim of counseling, there are many sources of error that would affect this criterion. Inheritance of money with a subsequent rise in income is one; vast differences between occupations is another. (As we shall see later, the average M.D. makes over twice as much as the average Ph.D.)

Still, it is argued here, in our current society there is a fairly sizeable relationship between income and achievement. The man who is achieving in his occupation is likely to be one of the better paid members of the occupation, whether or not it is important to him. And it is important to most men. Even in the academic world which prides itself on lack of materialism, the professor who is being paid less than someone he considers less competent usually takes whatever steps he can to correct the situation.

Perhaps the best argument for the use of income as a measure of success is that, in an informal way, most people consider it just that.

The use of the *husband's* income as a measure of the wife's achievements is another matter. This introduces another source of error, probably an overwhelming one. The counselor who would be uneasy about using the client's future income to measure his counseling effectiveness would no doubt become apoplectic at the use of the client's future husband's income as an index.

However, data for both sexes are presented in the following discussion. While more emphasis should be placed on the comparison between counseled and non-counseled males, the family incomes of the women are also intrinsically interesting. The income reported is total family income, including spouse's income, rental income, investment income, and so forth; usually the husband's salary accounted for the largest portion.

For the counseled males, annual incomes ranged from $1600 to $150,000, with a median of $14,670. For the non-counseled males, the range was from $4000 to $70,000, with a median of $13,500. Although recognizing that it reveals an undesirable lack of scientific objectivity, this investigator must confess that it pains him to report that this $1200 difference in median income was not statistically significant. In the combined distribution, 53 per cent of the counseled group were above the median, compared with 47 per cent of the non-counseled. The groups were almost identical.

For the counseled females, the family income (mostly the husband's salary) ranged from $1500 to $200,000, with a median of $13,300. For the non-counseled females, the range was from $4900 to $100,000, with a median of $13,000. This difference was neither statistically nor practically significant.

For a finer comparison between the counseled and non-counseled students, each group was broken down into the different degree levels, and the median for each group is presented in Table 40. Although the two largest categories, those of no degree and B.A. degree, show differences in favor of the counseled group, the trend was not consistent and none of the differences was statistically significant.

As was suggested earlier, there were wide differences between the degrees, and these are apparent in the table.

TABLE 40.   *Income by Degree Levels within Each Group*

| | Counseled | | Non-counseled | | Total | |
	N	Median	N	Median	N	Median
Men						
None	43	14,180	47	11,500	90	11,830
B.A.	74	13,000	41	12,870	115	13,000
M.A.	20	14,000	7	19,000	27	14,600
D.D.S.	3	21,000	3	18,000	6	18,500
L.L.B.	14	17,250	7	23,000	21	17,250
M.D.	10	25,500	16	37,000	26	29,500
Ph.D.	12	13,500	4	17,500	16	14,250
Women						
None	71	13,300	63	14,720	134	13,930
B.A.	92	13,500	48	12,100	140	12,810
M.A.	13	13,520	6	8,550	19	9,830
Ph.D.	3	8,500	0	--	3	8,500

It is difficult to know what to say about the family incomes of the women and, for the most part, the interpretation will be left up to the reader. One trend will be pointed out. As Table 40 indicates, there was a distinct inverse relationship between women's educational level and income. The higher the degree, the lower the income. The explanation for this, not apparent in the table, concerns the frequency of marriage among women of various educational levels. The higher the degree, the greater the probability that the woman was not married. For the single woman, the income figure includes only her own salary and, as women are clearly discriminated against in this area, the lower median income reflected this higher proportion of single women.

AN ULTIMATE CRITERION FOR COUNSELING RESEARCH

There is no more vexing problem in counseling research than that of the ultimate criterion. It has drawn a great deal of attention from professionals in the field, although seemingly more speculation has been produced than evidence. Many counseling psychologists can claim to have discussed the issue in print though, regrettably, only a much smaller proportion has added any real knowledge.

In these discussions of counseling outcomes, there is frequently some comment that the selection of an ultimate criterion requires a value judgment on someone's part, and the discussants at this point seem to veer in one of two directions. One group feels the case is hopeless because counselors should not make value judgments; the other, a smaller group, believes someone should be making these judgments and doing some research about the effect of them.

This project has taken the second direction. In the work reported in this section, an attempt was made to draw together all achievement data into one subjective rating. This involved the development of a rating scale, the application of that scale to the individuals in this study, and evaluation of the results. As this was a sizeable study in itself, considerable detail is presented to explain the rationale and methodology.

Of course, any attempt to develop a single measure of success or achievement faces the pitfall of individual variation in goals. Success to some men means fame and fortune; to others, fame is sufficient; while to a few, fortune in anonymity is to be preferred. There are others who seek neither of these but prefer rather a calm, contemplative life, free of the pressures that accompany financial and social success. Finally, there are those who have given up achieving any of the above and are, as Thoreau said, simply "living lives of quiet desperation."

With this in mind, it was perhaps foolhardy to attempt to rate everyone on the same criteria of accomplishment. Yet we tried. The scale of accomplishments finally developed—called "contribution to society"—may represent, more than anything else, the investigator's personal values, but it also certainly has much in common with widely accepted criteria of achievement. Perhaps its most controversial aspect is the complete disregard of any emphasis on the individual's internal satisfaction and happiness; however, results in those areas were studied and reported earlier. This section restricts itself to achievement, with or without satisfaction.

"CONTRIBUTION TO SOCIETY" SCALE

This rating scale had five points. Those points, including short descriptions of "typical" individuals for each category, are detailed here.

Men's Rating Scale

5—Highest Rating. Very valuable asset to our society. Contributing leadership in a high place or substantial achievement in literary, scientific, political, or similar areas. Possible examples are U.S. Congressmen, outstanding literary figures, creative research scientists, and outstanding business leaders. In general, people who are recognized for unusual personal achievement of value to society.

The individual does not have to be in a "social service" occupation. Outstanding businessmen certainly can be rated here if it is clear that, through their administrative duties or their community involvement, they are valuable to society. In general, anyone making over $50,000 would be a prime candidate for this category. Usually earnings of this magnitude (if legal) indicate skills valued by our society. Perhaps 5 to 10 percent of the group will rate here.

4—Substantial Contributors. Individuals who are making less spectacular, but still very worthwhile contributions. . . . People whose occupation almost assures a valuable contribution, such as doctors, lawyers, college professors, higher level business people. But there must be some service to others. The doctor who has no community involvement or research output, the college professor who does nothing more than teach, the businessman in the middle echelon who recognizes no need to contribute outside of his company *does not* belong in this group. Around 25 percent might rate this category.

3—The Solid Middle of College Educated Men. Men who perform fairly important jobs in a responsible manner, but where there is no evidence of anything outstanding either on or off the job. There is much value in what they contribute but it comes more from the adequate performance of the job than it does from the individual himself. Possible examples are teachers, small businessmen, the middle ranks of the military, etc. About 45 percent of the group.

2—The Solid Middle of the American Citizenry. These are people whose major contributions are those of the average American citizen. They do their jobs, raise decent families, stay out of trouble. They don't contribute to others, but neither do they generate grief. Perhaps some good stereotypes are the conscientious production worker, the capable Army sergeant, the dependable clerk. About 20 percent of the group.

1—The Burdens. Individuals who depend on society or others for their existence, or who cause a great deal of trouble. Usually includes chronic unemployed, the lawbreaker, the alcoholic. Probably less than 5 percent in this group.

Women's Rating Scale

5—Very Outstanding Women. Women making unusual contributions vocationally, probably all Ph.D.s and M.D.s. Also women with very outstanding records of community service. Wives of men who rate in Category 5 of the men's scale are prime candidates for this category—

also women with very outstanding children. Perhaps 5 to 10 percent of the group will rate here.

    4—Valuable Contributors. Homemakers involved in more than the average amount of volunteer activities—also those whose children have an outstanding record. Includes single women or working married women in occupations which are more than routine, teachers and nurses as opposed to clerical occupations. For a working mother to be placed in this category, there would have to be evidence that her family is not suffering because of her employment. Women with husbands in professional or higher level managerial positions would probably rank no lower than this unless their days were devoted exclusively to golf and bridge. About 25 percent might rate this category.

    3—Average College Educated Women. The average homemaker with average children who have average problems. The single woman or employed married woman whose occupation is of a more routine nature. Also, the working mother whose job is more than routine but whose children seem to have a number of problems. Women in this category would normally be making mild contributions to community activities, i.e., a few hours for the church, or PTA, etc. About 45 percent of the group.

    2—"Just a Housewife." Includes women who give evidence that they or their families are doing little more than just getting by from day to day. No community involvement, husband has a routine job, children at best are average and maybe have some problems. Might include women having marital problems. About 20 percent of the group would perhaps fall into this category.

    1—The Burdens. Women dependent on others, contributing to no one. Single, unemployed women. The divorcee living on alimony (unless she is caring for a family). Others who appear to be a burden to society. Probably less than 5 percent in this group.

Along with these rating scales, each rater was given the following set of instructions:

    Following are the guidelines I would like you to follow in rating these individuals. They include a number of value judgments that some of you may not agree with, but I hope that for these purposes, you will agree to step into my frame of reference. I have many qualms myself, but the only way to avoid any mistakes is to do nothing, and that seems even less fruitful.

    Briefly, these scales embody the "Protestant Ethic." They assume that personal achievement and contribution to community, both through occupational and extra-vocational channels are good; that a passive, bland life consisting of a 40 hour-a-week job, TV, and the family is bad. I would emphasize the achievement orientation, and achievement should be defined broadly. Any individual who is highly successful in his occupation, whether that occupation be professional, managerial, military, literary, political, or whatever should be rated highly.

    The scales are clearly related to both the hierarchy of occupations and the socio-economic ladder and this is precisely what I want. For a man, his occupation is his greatest outlet for contributing to the common good and, with few exceptions, individuals in higher level jobs contribute more than those in lower level ones. For a woman, the major outlet is her family and, whenever possible, she should be judged on that point first, using data on her husband's and children's accomplishments.

    Excellence. Unfortunately, the information seldom gives any direct evidence of the man's quality of performance. For example, it is difficult, probably impossible, to determine if a man is a good dentist from the data we have. However in some cases, by looking at the promotion records, by knowing the quality of individuals usually working at that job or for that employer (for example, Harvard University), by reading between the lines, it will be possible to infer some excellence attributable to the person. In those cases, you should consider raising the rating over what it might be otherwise.

Environment. The individual saddled with physical disability, the wife married to a husband whose job requires frequent moves with the attendant disruption, the mother with a very large family, the widow or widower raising a young family, must be rated more charitably.

Motivation and Internal Happiness. For the purpose of this rating, the person's internal feelings are of little consequence. A man living on a desert island, completely happy and at peace with himself, would rank very low on this scale. He is not contributing. He would not be at the bottom solely because he isn't dependent on others. The motivations of the individual are equally unimportant. A man may be a doctor (or a company president) mostly for money, but his contribution is still great. Another individual, strongly motivated to help others, might be a rural pastor making only a modest contribution to a very small congregation; his contribution would likely be less than that of a money-hungry professional man.

Black Marks. A few of these people have sizeable blots on their records of the type that society frowns upon. Divorce is the most frequent and is probably the most frequently excused. Imprisonment, abortion, alcoholism are less frequent and more severely censured. I'm not sure how much weight should be given to these aspects of the individual's total life, but I think they should be used as indicants for further probing. A person should not be rated lower solely on a single event unless there is evidence of other problems.

Women. The major variables making up the women's scale are children, home and husband. A woman with a very successful husband is an excellent candidate for a high rating, particularly when there is evidence that she has had a hand in the success. While it makes me uncomfortable to hang the rating of a woman on the pegs of her husband's and children's accomplishments, I see no other solution. Of course, her community activities are very important also. The occupational variable for women is covered fairly well in the rating scale itself.

Economic or Business Success. In this framework, an individual who has succeeded in the business world is to be rated highly.

Personal Stability. The individual's emotional stability should not be considered directly; it should enter in only when it is clear that the individual's occupation or family are being affected. For the purposes of this rating, individuals with long histories of institutional confinement will be considered to be burdens on society.

One informal comment should be made about this scale. The reader may have noted the emphasis on material success; financial gains especially were pointed out as praiseworthy. This was done in the hopes of offsetting in the raters—academic people all—the slight tendency in the academic world to belittle accomplishments in the business world (which is very little different from the analogous attitude in the business world toward academic achievements). There was little danger that these raters would overlook achievements in intellectual or social service areas, and I wanted to make sure that they also recognized achievements in other areas. This attitude should not be exaggerated, but if there is doubt that it exists, ask an academician how impressed he is by a successful campaign to sell more crunchy peanut butter, or ask the businessman how impressed he is by an article published in the "Evergreen Review." The values are different, but here they were forced into the same scale.

RATERS

Each person was rated on this scale by three psychologists working independently. Sixteen raters participated in this phase, all faculty members of the University of Minnesota, either in the Counseling Bureau or the Department of Psychology. Thirteen of them had Ph.D.s and the group had a median of ten years of counseling and research experience.*

INFORMATION USED IN RATINGS

To assist them in making the rating, the raters were given all of the information available on each person with the following exceptions: (1) any material from the Williamson-Bordin study, (2) test scores or grades, (3) Work Satisfaction Questionnaire, and (4) whether they were counseled or non-counseled.

Virtually everyone still alive was rated. For 600 individuals, both the questionnaire and interview notes were available to the raters; for another 16, the questionnaire; and for another 51, the interview notes. For the remaining 49, a credit report from the Retail Credit Association was used. These last reports were secured on all individuals declining to furnish information for this study. While this may have been a devious procedure, it was justified on the following grounds: Many of those refusing to cooperate in this study were obviously among the most unsuccessful individuals. It seemed unwise to eliminate this group from the study, so the only available channel of information was used.

RELIABILITY OF THE RATINGS

Each person was rated three times by raters working independently. Initially, in slightly over 3 percent of the cases, the

* I am indebted to the following for help in making these ratings: Emanuel Berger, Alice Christian, Rene Dawes, Marvin Dunnette, Patricia Faunce, Laurine Fitzgerald, Vivian Hewer, Al Hood, Lloyd Lofquist, Cornelia McCune, Jack Merwin, Gerhard Neubeck, Al Raygor, Ruth Roberts, Don Watley, Lenore White Harmon.

raters differed by two or more points. In these instances, the materials were returned to them and they were asked to review their decision. This re-rating brought all raters within one point of each other. In Table 41, which reports the total distribution of ratings, the degree of agreement can be seen. Ratings of 3, 6, 9, 12, and 15 represent cases of perfect agreement among the raters. (A rating of 15, for example, meant that each of the three raters gave the individual a rating of 5.)

TABLE 41.   *Distributions of "Contribution to Society" Rating for Counseled and Non-counseled Groups*

Total Score	Ratings	Men		Women		Total	
		Counseled Percent	Non-counseled Percent	Counseled Percent	Non-counseled Percent	Counseled Percent	Non-counseled Percent
15	5, 5, 5	3	1	2	0	2	0
14	5, 5, 4	6	3	4	3	5	3
13	5, 4, 4	7	6	8	11	7	8
12	4, 4, 4	16	14	16	15	16	14
11	4, 4, 3	18	12	20	17	19	14
10	4, 3, 3	13	16	19	17	16	16
9	3, 3, 3	16	28	16	17	16	22
8	3, 3, 2	7	11	6	7	7	9
7	3, 2, 2	4	5	5	7	4	6
6	2, 2, 2	7	6	4	5	6	5
5	2, 2, 1	2	0	0	1	1	1
4	2, 1, 1	1	0	0	0	0	0
3	1, 1, 1	1	0	1	0	1	0
	N	217	148	210	149	427	297
	Mean	10.15	9.84	10.30	10.15	10.22	9.99
	S.D.	2.48	1.98	2.15	2.10	2.33	2.05
	t-test	Not significant		Not significant		Not significant	

There was perfect agreement in 299 of the 724 cases, about 41 percent. In the remaining 59 percent, two raters agreed and the third deviated by one point. This reliability seems satisfactory, particularly as there probably were subjects who deserved to be rated higher than, say, two and lower than three. Allowing this one point deviancy might have increased the validity slightly, even though it lowered the percentage of perfect agreement.

RESULTS

The results of the ratings are reported in Table 41 for the counseled and non-counseled group within each sex. While the differences were all in favor of the counseled students, none of them was statistically significant.

Because this comparison was one of the most crucial ones in this study, a further more powerful statistical test was conducted, using only the matched pairs from the original Williamson-Bordin group. These were the pairs of students, one counseled, the other not, matched on ability and background variables in the study done 25 years earlier. A matched-pair t-test was run for both sexes, using the differences between pairs on this rating scale.

For the 123 pairs of males, the average difference, in favor of the counseled group, was 0.58 and the $SE_{diff} = .27$. Thus the $CR = 2.15$, indicating a difference significant at the 5 percent level. For the 121 pairs of females, the average difference was 0.15, the $SE_{diff} = .27$, the $CR = 0.52$; thus, there was no significant difference between the counseled and non-counseled women.

The counseled men rated significantly higher on this criterion, but is this an important finding? Is six-tenths of a point on a 13 point scale a practical difference? This is a subjective judgment that cannot be answered with data. Perhaps the main point is that a detectable difference has been found 25 years later between counseled and non-counseled men, one that is large enough so we can be fairly confident that it did not arise by chance. Moreover, this observed difference probably represents a lower limit of the real difference since the gross measures used, the lack of an adequate control group, and the random sources of error introduced by 25 years would tend to obscure the true effect of counseling.

That even the slightest difference appeared on such a gross measure must be considered most surprising and, to the counseling profession, most gratifying.

HIGHEST AND LOWEST RATED INDIVIDUALS

It may be informative to discuss briefly the characteristics of those rated at each extreme on this scale although, to preserve the anonymity of the individuals, the information presented must be sketchy.

There were 40 people given the highest rating, 5, and six given the lowest rating, 1, by at least two of the three raters. Of the 11 rated highest by all three raters, 10 of them were counseled. Of the 6 rated lowest, all were counseled. Counseling may have helped the first 10 get where they are today, but it certainly did not prevent the last 6 from making a considerable mess of their lives, although, from the counseling case notes, some of each group were well on their way to these ends 25 years ago.

Among the 40 individuals rated highly were six company presidents or vice-presidents, two men in advertising or public relations posts, and a few from the higher middle ranks of large corporations. From the academic world came five college professors, an assistant dean, and two coaches. There were a few self-employed professional people, two M.D.s and three people in public administration positions, one a former state governor.

Among the highly rated women, about half were housewives, married to very successful husbands, raising fine families. The employed women rated highly included three college professors and two women in public administrative jobs. No business woman merited this top rating in the eyes of the raters.

As was to be expected, the average income of these high-ranking individuals was substantial. The median income was $27,000, with 30 percent making $50,000 or more. The range was from $4000 to $200,000, with as many making over $100,000 as under $10,000, four of each. That is a substantial range of income among a group all rated as outstanding contributors to our society.

Among the six lowest ratings, not a single one was gainfully employed and at least three of the six apparently never had been since leaving college. Five of the six had some severe adjustment problems, and no data were available on this point for the sixth. With one possible exception, all of them were dependent on someone else for support, usually their parents.

ADULT ACHIEVEMENT AND FOLLOWING THE COUNSELOR'S ADVICE

One further refined analysis was done. The ratings of counseled students who followed the counselor's advice 25 years ago were compared with the ratings of counseled students who did not. This cooperation rating was discussed earlier on page 76. For this analysis, the two lowest categories were combined (Table 42).

TABLE 42. *"Contribution to Society" Ratings between Students Who Closely Followed the Counselor's Advice and Those Who Did Not*

	Men			Women		
	N	Mean	S.D.	N	Mean	S.D.
Followed advice	116	10.34	2.37	116	10.72	2.04
Did not	62	9.95	2.36	63	9.49	2.16
t-test	Not significant			p<.001		

Women who followed the counselor's advice have achieved more than women who did not. For the men, the difference was not significant, but it was in the proper direction.

CORRELATION WITH OTHER MEASURES

This measure of success was also correlated with other variables used in this study and the resulting correlations above .20 are reported in Table 43. The numbers used in establishing the correlation varied because of missing data but were roughly 300 for each sex. Thus, for each group, correlations of .20 were safely larger than those that might arise by chance.

TABLE 43. *Correlations between "Contribution to Society" Scale and Other Variables**

MALES Variables	Correlations	FEMALES Variables	Correlations
Current family income	.49+	Current family income	.35+
Total Work Satisfaction Scale	.47	"Ladder" Scale	.29+
Occupational satisfaction	.45	Total Work Satisfaction Scale	.27
Job satisfaction	.40	Occupational satisfaction	.26
Interviewer rating of affluence	.36	Job satisfaction	.23
College grade point average	.29	Interviewer rating of affluence	.26
"Ladder" Scale	.24+	MSAT	.25
High school rank	.23	High school rank	.24
MSAT	.22	College grade point average	.23
Williamson-Bordin rating of adjustment 25 years ago	.18	Williamson-Bordin rating of adjustment 25 years ago	.20
SVIB Scales		SVIB Scales	
Occupational level	.30	Physician	.22
City school superintendent	.27	Social science teacher	.22
Specialization level	.26	Psychologist	.21
Lawyer	.26	Librarian	.20
Public administrator	.22	Buyer	- .20
Psychologist	.20	Office worker	- .21
Accountant	- .20	Steno-secretary	- .21
Aviator	- .20		
Farmer	- .23		
Industrial arts teacher	- .24		
Office man	- .25		
Policeman	- .25		
Printer	- .27		
Carpenter	- .33		

*Only correlations > .20 are reported.
+Included in materials used by raters.

Though all of the correlations were low, the general thread of achievement ran through them. Prior college achievement, high school achievement, test scores, and the earlier rating of adjustment made in the Williamson-Bordin study all correlated positively with current achievement. This rating was also correlated positively with both work satisfaction, and general satisfaction with life as measured by the "ladder" scale.

The highest correlation for both sexes was with current income, but this was probably an inflated figure since this information was included in the materials used by the raters.

The correlations with the scales on the Strong Vocational Interest Blank are also reported. For both sexes, social service interests were positively related to this rating, business and skilled trades interests were negatively related.

CONCLUSIONS

What conclusions and implications are suggested by the preceding data?

First, it is clear that those students who received counseling fared better during college than the non-counseled students. They earned better grades, more and higher honors, more degrees, and participated more in campus life. Further, those students who paid the most attention to the counseling profited most.

Second, these data suggest that there was a very mild, but distinguishable, difference between counseled and non-counseled students 25 years later, especially among the men. Considering the problems of measurement, of experimental design, and the likelihood that neither the counselor nor the student 25 years ago were thinking in terms of the outcomes reported here, this investigator would again emphasize the remarkable fact that any difference appeared.

Third, in general, the major conclusion seems to be that counseling did indeed exert a beneficial effect on the student's achievement. This effect was most apparent on immediate criteria such as grades and graduation but, although it withered considerably, it did not completely disappear during the intervening 25 years. This trend is not surprising. Counselors are more effective in dealing with problems immediately at hand and, for college students, these frequently concern grades and graduation.

Extrapolating from these results and others reported in the chapter dealing with review of the literature, it is quite likely that counselors working with adults could improve performance on whatever *immediate* achievement measures the counselors and adults agreed were important. But to ask the counselor to achieve far-reaching, long-term effects working with the teen-ager 25 years earlier is demanding more than even the most fundamental religions require of the Almighty Himself, as they at least grant Him the opportunity to intervene occasionally in the affairs of the adult. The counselor cannot do that, but these data show that he can help the student to find solutions to situations at hand and, by this, help him to make more of his life eventually.

CHAPTER NINE

WHAT THEY SAY ABOUT
THEIR COUNSELING
TWENTY-FIVE YEARS LATER

The student's opinion of his former counseling is not necessarily crucial or even relevant to the question of whether the counseling was effective. The value of a counseling program is not dependent upon reminiscence since even students who do not remember talking with a counselor may have been helped in ways they do not appreciate. Nevertheless, these comments of former counselees should be studied for at least two reasons: one, most counselors would be quite disturbed if their clients had nothing good to say about the counseling or, perhaps worse, if none of them remembered it; second, by studying the opinions of these former counselees, ways may be found to improve current counseling techniques.

In addition, there is an inherent fascination in these reports, stretching over 25 years, for the counselor who is continually wondering if he is making any impact on the lives of the young people he works with. Whatever they may think of them, whatever implications they may draw from them, most counselors will find these comments interesting.

Biases can creep into studies of this kind in several ways. People are agreeable, for the most part, and they are prone to tell the researcher what they think he wants to hear. Because of this, we took many pains to mask the real nature of this project from the participants. If they had been aware that this was a follow-up of counseling effectiveness, they might well have been more complimentary. Instead, they were told that it was a follow-up study of college students who had entered college during the depression, and this was no misstatement, for it indeed was that.

In this study, no letterhead stationery was used, no titles were used in signing letters, and the interview and questionnaire materials were designed so that the questions on counseling were buried among other more general material concerned with the entire collegiate experience.

There is no way of evaluating whether this masking was successful; the investigator can only hope that it was.

Another source of possible bias was in the interviewers. They took notes during the interview, and these notes were used for the results presented in this chapter. As these notes were condensations of longer conversations, it is possible that some kind of selectivity crept into the comments that the interviewers wrote down. Possibly they reported only the compliments and glossed over the criticisms. This was no problem in about half of the interviews, the ones done outside Minneapolis, as these interviewers were told no more about the project than the participants. However, for the half of the interviews conducted in the Twin Cities, the interviewer was either a graduate student working as a research assistant on the project or the investigator, himself. The only safeguard here was to stress to the interviewers the possibility of this bias and hope they would guard against it. Also, of course, whether the person was a counseled or a control student was concealed from the interviewer as long as possible, but presumably this would come out in the interview.

Thus, for half of the interviews, the only safeguard was an awareness of the possibility of bias. Hopefully, this was sufficient to avoid any gross errors.

A visual check of the distribution of ratings made by the Twin City interviewers versus those made by the non-Twin City interviewers indicated these two distributions were virtually identical, a reassuring finding. The data taken from the questionnaires were, of course, completely free of this possible bias.

COMMENTS FROM THE QUESTIONNAIRE

On the questionnaire, the subjects were asked to check the importance of various influences on their career decisions. Those data are presented in Table 44.

TABLE 44. *Percent of Counseled and Non-counseled Students Indicating Importance of Various Sources of Guidance*

	Counseled (N = 367)					Non-counseled (N = 250)				
	Very Important	Somewhat Important	Unimportant	Rec'd None	No Response	Very Important	Somewhat Important	Unimportant	Rec'd None	No Response
Vocational or psychological tests	17	37	34	9	2	5	12	34	44	5
Discussions with academic adviser	8	24	34	29	5	4	18	20	52	5
Discussions with faculty members other than adviser	10	22	23	39	6	6	20	20	50	5
Advice from parents	17	36	24	20	3	20	42	19	16	4
Interviews with a professional psychological or vocational counselor	13	18	25	38	6	5	5	8	77	5
High school teacher	6	16	30	42	6	8	21	21	45	4

Two trends are worth noting in this table. First, the counseled students cited all kinds of collegiate guidance as more important than did the non-counseled students, while the non-counseled students cited off-campus guidance sources (parents and high school teachers) as most important. To the extent that the counseling kept the counseled students in school longer, helped them find a curriculum in which they would be happy and successful, and suggested other faculty for them to talk to, it had some influence on their contacts with other faculty. As we have already seen, the counseled students were more often graduated, won more scholastic honors, earned higher grades, participated more often in campus activities, and were more often elected to student offices. Clearly, they were more involved in campus life and had more opportunities for all kinds of contacts. This, of course, was a two-way street. The more contact they had with faculty and counselors, the more they were influenced. Thus, the student benefited and achieved more through this increased stimulation.

The second major trend in the table shows that, among the counseled students, parents and vocational tests were listed as the most influential. The professional counselor came in a weak third, along with faculty adviser, and other faculty members. The students remembered the tests more vividly than they did the counseling.

Several factors may be involved here. Certainly, counseling was very test-oriented at Minnesota then, and it may not be too inaccurate in some cases for the student to remember his counseling as simply taking tests and having the results interpreted to him. Beyond this, taking a psychological test is a more unique stimulus than talking with a faculty member about your plans and would probably be remembered more clearly.

Finally, it may be that students simply paid more attention to the tests than anything else in making up their minds about their next course of action.

One other figure in the table needs elaboration. Among the counseled, 38 percent said they never had any interviews with a counselor. In some cases this may have been due to confusion on their part as to exactly who was a counselor. To discriminate between a faculty adviser, a faculty counselor, and other faculty members at a distance of 25 years is not the simplest task, especially if your faculty adviser also happened to be a professional psychologist. Some of the 32 percent of counseled students who cited "academic adviser" as an important source of help may have been referring to the counseling.

Also, these counseled students were selected for this study because they were initially counseled either before entering the

University or very early in their freshman year, frequently during the orientation period. It may be that they simply accepted it as part of that procedure.

The old case notes were reviewed for those individuals who forgot they were ever counseled, and no particular trend could be found to explain why they should forget while others remembered. One student had changed his name and drastically changed his life since then, another had been referred to counseling because of some severe trouble he was in. These situations might have affected their memories. But similar instances were found among those who did remember. That two-thirds remembered is reassuring; that one-third forgot is puzzling.

Among the non-counseled were several people (5 to 10 percent) who said that tests and counseling were influential in their decisions. About half of these individuals, those living in the Twin Cities, were contacted by phone and asked further about this. The group who indicated that tests were influential said they had taken the tests in a variety of situations: psychology courses, military service, as job applicants, and so forth, and they had paid some attention to the results in pondering their careers. Most of those checking the "interviews with a professional counselor" as important said they apparently had confused it with their regular academic adviser, though a few reported they had received some helpful guidance from sources other than the Counseling Bureau, such as a friendly Dean or another member of the Psychology Department, or perhaps a counselor in another school.

It could be argued that these individuals should have been moved into the counseled group for the analyses of this report. After some indecision this was not done, mainly for two reasons. First, it was difficult to draw the line between those who should be moved and those who should not. For example, is taking tests in an employment situation and receiving the results synonymous with counseling? Second, the actual number of cases in question was quite small and would not have materially affected the results anyway. (The 15 non-counseled students most likely to have been moved to the counseled group rated slightly higher on the "contribution to society" measure than their matched mates. Thus, if they had been moved, it would have made the difference in favor of the counseled students even larger.)

COMMENTS FROM THE INTERVIEW

The remaining data in this chapter are based on comments made by the participants during the interview.

TABLE 45. *Percent of Counseled Students Who Mentioned Counseling at Various Points in the Interview*

Questions	Percent Who Mentioned Counseling	Cummulative Percent Who Mentioned Counseling
How did you happen to enter your present occupation?	5	5
What influenced you in choosing your present occupation?	3	8
Do you remember any one person who was particularly influential in advising you about which occupation you should enter?	8	16
Did you ever receive any formal vocational counseling while you were in college?	53	69
Have you ever had any contact with the University Testing Bureau or Student Counseling Bureau at the University of Minnesota?	18	87
Remainder	13	100
	100	

In the interview, we wanted to ascertain from the former students how much influence they thought the counseling had had on their lives but did not want to ask the question bluntly, as there was the considerable danger that they would play the game too well and tell us something like, "Oh, it was the greatest thing that ever happened to me." To avoid that, we started with open-ended questions and worked into the specific details of the counseling. The series of questions is listed in Table 45.

After each question is listed the percentage of people who mentioned at that point in the interview that counseling was influential on their career choice. The table should be read as follows: When asked how they happened to enter their occupation, 5 percent listed counseling as the most important reason. When asked the next question, "What influenced you . . . ," another 3 percent mentioned counseling.

These data show that, in response to open-ended questions, about one-sixth of the counseled students mentioned counseling as a very significant influence on their career choice.

Another half, when asked directly, remembered being counseled.

Another 18 percent reported they had never received any formal vocational counseling but that they had had some contact with the Student Counseling Bureau (or University Testing Bureau as it was then called), usually commenting that they took some tests there to help them decide what to major in.

Finally, 13 percent of the counseled students who, according to University records, had had at least one formal interview with a counselor, said, "No, I never received any counseling," or "No, I never had any contact with the Student Counseling Bureau."

Thus, an overwhelming majority of the counseled students remembered the counseling, although it may have been only one or two hours 25 years ago.

A more crucial question is, did they remember it as being helpful?

The 87 percent who remembered being counseled were asked the following three questions:

Do you remember what the counselor said?

Did it have any influence on your life?

Do you think the counseling was helpful?

With the use of the notes taken by the interviewer, each person's comments were categorized roughly as shown in Table 46. While this categorization unfortunately destroyed the personal quality of the comments, many of which were fascinating, it does impose some meaningful structure on an otherwise jumbled set of statements.

The comments have been split into seven categories, ranging from "very favorable" to "very unfavorable" according to the general tone of the comments. Within each of the seven broad categories, sub-categories have been described to give a better idea of the comments. It should be emphasized that the phrasing is that of the investigators; many of the comments were expressed in more vivid, eloquent language.

As Table 46 shows, a considerable majority of people felt that the counseling had been helpful. Almost three-fourths of the group fell on the favorable side of the median, with one-fourth in the very favorable category. Twenty percent fell on the unfavorable side of the midpoint, with only 4 percent in the very unfavorable category. Among this last group were a few individuals with both low test scores and low high school grades; it is apparent that the counselor steered them away from a field in which they very likely would have failed.

For example, one fellow, who scored in the bottom fourth of the freshman class on the entrance examination, said, "I had always planned on either law or engineering but the counselor convinced me I should enter a business course. If I hadn't listened to him, I'd be in one of the professions now."

Following are a few other quotes, paraphrased from the inter-

TABLE 46. *Comments about Counseling*

Categories	N	Percent
Very favorable		
The counselor suggested specific change of curriculum and I did and I'm glad	18	4
The counselor showed me a new way of thinking — which issues I should consider in planning career, etc.	14	4
General help — somebody paid attention to me — counseling content itself not important	12	3
The counselor helped me solve a specific, non-vocational problem (parental dispute, personality problem, etc.)	5	1
The counselor suggested a specific course of action and I followed suggestion, and I'm happy that I did	62	16
Sub-total:	111	28
Favorable		
The counselor confirmed what I already thought and this was reassuring	53	14
Counseling was helpful but I didn't or couldn't follow it — now I wish I had	27	7
I chose not to follow advice but it was still helpful to have the benefits of his thinking	8	2
The counselor pointed out several things that I shouldn't do (Some went on — but never indicated what I should do)	7	2
The counselor assured me that I had the ability to do what I was planning	16	4
Sub-total:	111	29
Mildly favorable		
The counseling had little impact (but comments were generally positive)	36	9
The counseling was good but there was not enough of it — or it was not early enough — or it was too hurried	26	7
I was too mixed up and didn't listen to anyone then, but the counselor did try	2	-
Sub-total:	64	16

Table 46. Continued

Categories	N	Percent
Neutral feelings		
Yes, I was counseled but I don't remember anything at all about it	27	7
Sub-total:	27	7
Mildly unfavorable		
The counselor suggested a specific course of action and I did it but now I'm not sure it was wise	5	1
The counseling had little impact (but comments were generally negative)	6	2
I took some tests but no one ever explained the results to me	16	4
The counselor should have followed me up to see if I was doing okay	3	1
Sub-total:	30	8
Unfavorable		
The counselor was not directive enough — he didn't tell me what I should do	7	2
The counselor suggested something but I didn't have any confidence in him — or I didn't trust the tests — or the suggestion was completely unacceptable to me	10	2
The counselor confirmed what I already thought but this was no help — I already knew that	14	4
Sub-total:	31	8
Very unfavorable		
The counselor definitely steered me in the wrong direction — with subsequent harmful effects	12	3
The whole enterprise of psychological testing and counseling is ridiculous — psychologists have a very inflated opinion of their knowledge	3	1
Sub-total:	15	4
TOTAL:	389	100

viewer's notes. Usually it is quite apparent which category they were assigned to.

> "My choice of career was almost entirely due to E. G. Williamson. I went to the University expecting to go into medicine but he told me with my pattern of interests and abilities, I'd be better off in engineering. I have been continually happy that I made that change." (He is now director of a large engineering test center.)
> "I was thinking of majoring in journalism when I went to see the counselor. He told me that he thought this would be a good choice for me and this confirmation was reassuring."
> "I was thinking of majoring in journalism. The counselor said he thought this would be a good choice for me as my interests seemed to be in that direction. He was not much help—he didn't tell me anything I didn't already know."
> "When I came to the University, I was all mixed up. When I took those tests, I set out deliberately to falsify them. Then I knew I would really be crazy to accept any advice based on those results, so I ignored the counselor completely."

IMPLICATIONS

These are the data; what do they imply?

The most obvious theme is that most of these people look back on their counseling with favor. While many of them felt it was not so thorough and complete as they would have liked, the majority remembered it as beneficial.

Although this general feeling of satisfaction cannot be counted as proof in any rigorous sense, it should be reassuring to the hundreds of counselors working day in and day out without even this rudimentary feedback.

In this sense, the pleas of the non-counseled students were perhaps even more meaningful than the plaudits of the counseled. In answer to the question "What could the University have done differently that would have helped you more," the most common answer among the non-counseled students, given by 22 percent, was a request for some kind of counseling. (The most frequent answer among the counseled was a request for *better counseling*.) The greatest deficiency these former students saw in their collegiate career was a lack of adequate advising.

What further implications can be drawn that will help counselors to improve their techniques? I feel no special skill in interpreting these data for this purpose and a considerable attempt was made to describe the categories in Table 46 as fully as possible so that the reader could draw his own conclusions. Still, I have been closer to this information than anyone else and feel the responsibility to draw some conclusions from what these people had to say. The reader should be warned, however, that the following interpretative conclusions were drawn by a pragmatic psychometrician with very little counseling experience.

First, what these students sought and wanted most was a rather firm kind of advice. They did not want a counselor who was simply kind and accepting, who smiled and reflected back at them, "Ummm, so that's what you think?" They wanted advice, though to be sure they were expecting the advice to be based on firm knowledge. They wanted to talk with a professional person who had some measuring instruments—tests—that would tell them something about themselves. Further, they wanted to talk with someone who knew something about the practical world of jobs, who knew which curricular choices might lead to which careers, who knew where the rewards might lie for their type of person.

The point is that, primarily, these people had been seeking information and guidance. They had not been trying to develop their self-concept; they had not been trying to talk their way through a complicated set of Freudian entanglements. For the most part, they were trying to decide which curriculum and, eventually, which occupation was for them.

Of course, the kind of counseling these people received probably had something to do with their reactions toward it. The counseling, done by E. G. Williamson and his colleagues, was of a positive type and discussions of tests and jobs were important in this process. Undoubtedly, these methods had some effect on what the students reported as good and bad about their counseling. Still, this investigator heard so many of these people say, "If only someone had taken a firmer stand with me," "If only someone had given some direction to my efforts," that he cannot help but feel that most of these counselees would have been disappointed to find a counselor who refused to take an active role in helping them plan their subsequent course of action.

This does not mean that there were not some who wanted to talk through some sort of emotional entanglement. A small but significant percentage indicated that they were very mixed up, that they had sizable personal problems, and, as the comments show, the "satisfaction with counseling" rate was as high with these students as with the larger majority. The counselors were sensitive enough to detect these cases requiring more time and personal attention and, if the person's self report has any validity, were successful in dealing with them.

A second major theme, represented less well in the table of comments and expressed explicitly by only a few people, ran vaguely through a substantial number of interviews. At the expense of over-simplification, a blunt statement of it might be, "At some *critical point* in my college days, I wish somebody (a counselor) had approached me and helped me over a particular hurdle."

The point of criticality varied from person to person, but some generalities were visible. Perhaps it occurred during the quarter they were dropped from the University for grade deficiencies, or perhaps the quarter they dropped out for personal or financial reasons, or the quarter that their grade point average dropped from a comfortable 3.00 to 0.50 as a result of an earth-shattering (to them) breakup of a romance. As one man said, "If someone had just given me some encouragement to stick out that one bad quarter, I think I might have made it the rest of the way."

Several instances of successful counseling during these critical periods were noted to substantiate this trend. One counselee said, "The counselor convinced me that my financial situation, though pretty bad, was good enough to try one more quarter. I finished that one, then the next, and somehow finally graduated."

Other counseled students, while commenting that the counseling was helpful, said further, "The counselor should have followed me up a year later to see how I was doing, rather than just relying on that one-shot affair."

From comments of the above nature, I would suggest that counselors and student personnel workers make some attempt to predict critical points in the academic life cycle of the student, and then be aggressive in offering services to the student at those points. Any substantial, precipitous drop in grades or the failure to register for a current session when performance over past sessions has been good are only two examples of indications that all may not be well with the student. Leaving the initiative for making first contact in the hands of the student at this point is not the most effective way for counseling services to proceed.

Perhaps unsolicited testimonials have little place in a report that hopes to be scientific. Yet, in closing this chapter, the following letter from one of the counseled students who is now a faculty member of another university has some relevance.

> "I shall always remember the kindness and patience shown me when I first entered the University when I was neither emotionally or physically up to doing a good job. The services of the Testing Bureau and the counseling given me were invaluable. I only regret that we have nothing like that here for the students who enter with the need for help. . . ."

CHAPTER TEN

CONCLUSIONS
AND IMPLICATIONS

The following conclusions have been drawn from the research reported in the preceding pages:

1. The students who sought counseling were mildly different— on the average—from those who did not. They scored slightly higher on measures of academic potential, also slightly higher on measures of personal discomfort, and they more often were first-born.

2. Counseling was directly associated with success in the University (with academic potential held constant). The graduation rate among counseled students was one-fourth higher than among the non-counseled and the difference was even larger among the advanced degree winners. Also, the counseled students earned better grades, more and higher academic honors, more often participated in campus activities and more often were elected to offices in those activities.

3. Twenty-five years after counseling, the counseled students still were more successful and uncomfortable. Though both trends were apparent in both sexes, the first trend was more prominent among the men, the second among the women. Counseled men reported slightly higher incomes and have contributed more to society than the non-counseled men; counseled women more often reported anxiety, personal discomfort, and mild dissatisfaction than did the non-counseled women.

4. The point should be emphasized that the differences between the counseled and non-counseled students 25 years later were all very slight in degree. While the trends were consistent

and had some anchors in statistical significance, they were not large and impressive.

5. The former students' recollections about the counseling they had received 25 years earlier were favorable. Two-thirds of them remembered being counseled, and three-quarters of this group thought that it had been helpful. About eight percent remembered it as the most important influence on their career decisions.

Did the counseling cause these differences? There is no simple answer.

Clearly, differences did exist before counseling, and at least some of these persisted after counseling, mainly in the area of personal discomfort. If students seeking counseling are worried and anxious, shy and under-confident, and if the adult 25 years later reports essentially the same feelings, counseling cannot claim these feelings as outcomes, which is fortunate because most counselors would not want them anyway. Of course, neither can the counselor claim reduction in anxiety as an outcome. While realizing that the measures used in this study were much too gross to be able to demonstrate any small changes in these variables, this investigator nevertheless concludes that counseling had little effect on self-confidence and anxiety level. The students worried before they came and they worried after they left.

Further, there were no hints of any causal connections between these variables and the counseling, nor were there any introspective anecdotal comments reporting that the counselor had made the student feel less secure in some way.

However, the differences between groups on the achievement variables seemed to be a different matter. There are some reasons to believe that counseling affected those variables, particularly those concerned with academic performance. Several points illustrate this:

1. Differences in graduation rates appeared even though the groups had been matched on the only variables thus far shown to be related very highly to graduation, i.e., high school achievement and scholastic ability test scores.

2. The differences in graduation rates were greater when students who followed the counseling plan were compared with those who did not.

3. The differences in the graduation rates were greater among those with advanced degrees, and the characteristics of those degree winners indicated that counselors probably had some effect on the quality of students continuing on to graduate school, since the counseled graduate students proved to be more academically able than the non-counseled.

4. The self-reported anecdotes of the counseled students indicated that they thought this area of academic decision-making was the one in which the counselor was most helpful and had the most influence (though they did not always agree that it was beneficial).

While there are various alternative explanations for each of these findings, the most parsimonious explanation to account for all of them is the effectiveness of the counseling.

IMPLICATIONS

The major implications of these findings for the actual counseling process will have to be drawn by others with more counseling sophistication than this investigator. The type of counseling that went on at Minnesota while these students were here (1933 to 1940) was—from reading the case notes—simultaneously directive and client-centered, and vestiges of both approaches were found in the students' comments about their former counseling. One does not enter further into this area of discussion without a broad philosophic acquaintance with (and possible commitment to one of?) the various viewpoints represented.

However, the implications for providing some sort of counseling service to students are clearer. The students who were counseled clearly fared better as undergraduates than the non-counseled. Further, those who were counseled said it was helpful and wished that they had had more guidance. Those who did not receive any counseling reported—in retrospect—this as the greatest deficiency in the University's program. From both of these sources, one objective, the other subjective, the results support the value of these services.

Of course, these results alone are hardly dramatic enough to justify extensive counseling facilities; but this is a relative point since there are no data available to support unequivocally and dramatically ANY program of student services or, for that matter, any particular type of curriculum or instruction. Students are required to take orientation courses, to take 15 hours of a foreign language, to participate in physical education classes, to go to chapel, and sometimes even their daily attendance in class is required. They are expected to go to school three quarters, or two semesters, each year and to graduate in four years. Practically nothing done to them or required of them during that period has an established foundation of empirical fact stretching over a lengthy time period.

These statements are not made critically but simply to point out that decisions on how to treat students are usually made in the absence of knowledge or, at best, in the presence of knowledge stretching over a short time period.

Counseling is still best justified as a help to the student bewildered by the increasing complex maze of educational and occupational opportunities. In this maze, most institutions will recognize their responsibility to help the student to explore his potentials and possibilities in an orderly, systematic manner. The provision of professional people in counseling services is one way to achieve that, and it is a comforting fact that this method is supported by the data in this study, certainly over the short 4-year academic period and, in a milder way, over the lengthier span of a quarter of a century.

CHAPTER ELEVEN

CROSS-SECTIONAL AND LONGITUDINAL COMPARISONS OF SCHOLASTIC ABILITIES OVER TWENTY-FIVE YEARS

INTRODUCTION

To this point, this report has been concerned with the effect of counseling on the development of former students at the University of Minnesota. In the following chapters, two further aspects of their development are discussed: first, the development of scholastic aptitudes over time, including some comparisons with current students; and, second, the impact of political attitudes on vocational choice.

This chapter is concerned with two issues: First, how do college freshmen of the 1960's compare with those of the 1930's on college aptitude tests? Second, how well do freshmen of the 1930's, now about 45 years old, perform on current tests?

The comparison between freshmen of 25 years ago and freshmen of today is pertinent since there is a widely held opinion that, as more students are seeking a college education now, the intellectual qualities of incoming freshmen must be dropping. State universities are especially concerned as they see many top students from their states siphoned off by high-prestige liberal arts colleges, leaving them—so they suspect—with classes declining in ability. However, evidence is accumulating that suggests that college students today in a large state university are not inferior to students

109

of past decades (Berdie, Layton, Hagenah, and Swanson, 1962);
data in this chapter add to that evidence.

The second question posed "What happens to scholastic abilities as people grow older?" also has an answer rooted in persistent
popular opinion. Many people believe that individuals decline in
their mental capacities as they move into adulthood, roughly past
age 30. While there was some support for this view in the early
cross-sectional studies of mental abilities (Jones and Conrad, 1933;
Miles and Miles, 1932), several more recent longitudinal studies
such as Nancy Bayley's work (Bayley, 1955), Terman's study of
a gifted group (Terman and Oden, 1958), Owens' longitudinal
study of college freshmen (Owens, 1953), Charles' study of men-
tally retarded children over 15 years (Charles, 1953), and Swanson's study of bright high school seniors over a 25-year period
(Swanson, 1953) indicate that the decreases in mental capacity
found in the earlier cross-sectional studies were more likely attributable to the sampling methods used rather than to any actual
decline within the individual. The longitudinal studies over periods
of several years have shown no decline in mental abilities for age
groups up to the 50's.

On both issues raised above, the results reported here are reassuring. The cross-sectional comparison between college freshmen of
today versus those of the 1930's showed little difference between
the groups, while the longitudinal comparison between the individual's test performance as a college freshmen and his performance
as an adult showed a great difference in favor of the adult.

METHOD

Several groups of people were used, all students from the College of Science, Literature, and the Arts (SLA) of the University
of Minnesota.

THE CROSS-SECTIONAL GROUPS

The first group included the entire freshman classes of 1933
and 1936. For the 1933 class, results were available for the 1933
College Aptitude Test, Form AM (1933 CAT). For the 1936 class,
results were available for the 1936 American Council of Education
Examination (1936 ACE). These tests were completed during the
fall orientation program for entering freshmen.

The second group included freshmen who entered the University during the fall of 1962, roughly 25 years after the first group. During freshmen orientation, a random sample of approximately 500 students took the two tests mentioned above, the 1933 CAT and the 1936 ACE. Scores for these students were also available on the University's current entrance examination, the Minnesota Scholastic Aptitude Test (MSAT), a derivative of the Ohio series authored by Layton and Toops. Since this test was taken during the spring of the high school junior year, there was an 18 month difference between the MSAT and the other two tests.

Comparisons between this random sample and the entire 1962 class on both MSAT scores and High School Rank (HSR) are reported in Table 47. Neither difference was statistically significant; the sample was a representative one.

TABLE 47.   *Random Sample of 1962 Freshmen versus Entire Class on MSAT Scores and High School Rank*

	N	MSAT		HSR	
		M	S.D.	M	S.D.
Random sample 1962 freshmen	476	46.7	12.6	74.2	19.6
1962 Freshman class	3011	45.7	11.9	73.7	19.2

THE LONGITUDINAL GROUP

The third group were those who had entered the University as freshmen during the 1930's and who were retested in 1962, i.e., the participants in the study of counseling effectiveness reported in the earlier chapters. As part of that study, they were asked to take the MSAT, and those results are presented here.

The relevant descriptive data on this sample have been presented in the earlier chapters; generally, this group included 45 year old people who had entered the University of Minnesota about 25 years ago and who agreed to take a current college entrance examination. The group, predominantly urban dwellers living in 38 states and 9 countries, contained leaders in many areas: prominent public officials, well-known athletic coaches, bank presidents or vice-presidents, several college professors, company presidents, and also a few alcoholics and itinerants. Two-thirds of the group were college graduates.

These, then, were the three main groups used in these comparisons: the entire freshmen classes of 1933 and 1936, a random sample of 1962 freshmen, and a selected sample of 1933 to 1936 freshmen who were retested in 1962.

RESULTS AND DISCUSSION

1962 Freshmen versus 1933 to 1936 Freshmen

The first comparison was made between the freshman classes of the 1930's and the freshmen class of 1962. Those data are presented in Table 48.

TABLE 48. *Test Scores and High School Ranks for 1933 and 1936 Freshmen and 1962 Freshmen*

Percentile Points	1936 ACE		1933 CAT		High School Rank		
	1936 Freshmen	1962 Freshmen	1933 Freshmen	1962 Freshmen	1933 Freshmen	1936 Freshmen	1962 Freshmen
100	319+	329+	212+	207+			100
90	262	272	190	182	NOT AVAILABLE	NOT AVAILABLE	95
75	230	239	174	169			89
Median	197	201	154	152			78
25	162	173	128	132			61
10	137	150	102	109			45
1	99-	109-	71-	69-			17-
Mean	198	208	155	150	72	71	74
S.D.	48	47	30	29	23	24	20
N	1180	476	1193	476	1512	1050	476

All of the differences between the means in Table 48 are significant beyond the 1 percent level but, as the data show, not in the same direction. The 1936 ACE test and HSR slightly favored current freshmen while the 1933 CAT favored freshmen of the 30's.

One hypothesis as to why the two tests gave different results was suggested by inspection of the item content. The 1936 ACE contains vocabulary, numerical, and symbolic items while the 1933 CAT is strictly a vocabulary test. Probably vocabulary materials become obsolete faster than numerical or symbolic materials. If this occurs, current freshmen would be handicapped and would score relatively lower on the 1933 CAT than on the 1936 ACE.

A separate analysis of the subtests of the 1936 ACE gave mild support to this hypothesis. Though none of the differences was statistically significant, without exception the 1936 freshmen did better on the vocabulary subtests while the current freshmen did better on the numerical and symbolic subtests. Thus, the slight superiority of earlier freshmen on the 1933 CAT was probably due to item content.

From the data in Table 48, it is clear that today's freshmen are not inferior to freshmen of the 30's; in fact, they may be slightly superior. The increasing enrollment has not pushed quality down, at least in the Liberal Arts College at the University of Minnesota. (As nearly as can be determined, admissions standards were not a factor in this comparison as they have been constant over the past 25 years—admission of roughly the upper 60 percent of Minnesota high school graduates.)

One possible explanation of how quality can be maintained in the face of rising numbers is suggested in some findings of Berdie and Hood (1963). They compared Minnesota high school seniors of 1950 and 1961 and found that the increase in college attendance among the very top high school students was three times (14 percent) as high as the average increase (5 percent). Proportionately, more of the good students of Minnesota were going to college compared with a decade earlier. Possibly this was the result of the expansion and improvement of counseling facilities in Minnesota high schools, where some informal screening occurs when the student is making his post-high school plans.

Whatever the cause, the results are clear: though there are more of them, college freshmen of today are as capable as college freshmen of the 1930's.

ADULT PERFORMANCE OF 1933 TO 1936 FRESHMEN

How do freshmen of the mid-30's, now about 45 years old, do on current scholastic aptitude tests? Because this retested group was not randomly selected, it was first necessary to determine how atypical it was. Data relevant to that determination are given in

TABLE 49. *Twenty-five Year Retest Group versus Their Peers*

		CAT Percentile*		HSR Percentile	
	N	M	S.D.	M	S.D.
Williamson-Bordin group	768	63	25.0	73	23.0
1936 SLA freshmen	1050	63†	‡	71	23.5
Random sample 1933-1936					
SLA freshmen	713	57	26.7	68	24.5

* College Aptitude Test percentile based on all University of Minnesota freshmen.

† Percentile corresponding to raw score mean.

‡ Not available.

Table 49. Three groups are listed: first, the Williamson-Bordin group from the counseling effectiveness study, second, the entire Arts College freshman class of 1936, and third, a random sample of freshmen from 1933 to 1936 drawn with the same composition of sex and year of entry as the Williamson-Bordin sample.

While the differences were not large, they consistently favored the Williamson-Bordin group over either the entire single class or the sample drawn from the four classes. The Williamson-Bordin group was slightly superior, by roughly one-fourth to one-tenth of a standard deviation, to their peers.

This difference was increased slightly by the bias created by self-selection on the retest. Those who agreed to take the MSAT were slightly more able in their college years than those declining to participate. Table 50 compares the various subgroups on test scores, high school rank, and college grades from their student records of 25 years ago.

TABLE 50.   *MSAT Takers versus Non-takers in 25-Year Retest Group*

Groups	N	HSR Percentile		CAT Percentile		GPA*	
		M	S.D.	M	S.D.	M	S.D.
MSAT takers	634	74	22.3	63	24.9	2.17	.74
Refusals	97	72	24.1	58	26.0	2.12	.68
Unlocated	7	57	19.4	74	25.5	1.87	.67
Deceased	30	56	29.0	60	26.9	1.79	.79

* Based on undergraduate record (A = 4.0).

The most remarkable difference to appear in this chapter was generated by the comparison on the MSAT between the 45 year old retest group and current freshmen tested as 16 year old high school juniors. Those data are presented in Table 51.

These two groups differ by almost a full standard deviation, a far bigger difference than could be explained by the non-random

TABLE 51.   *Retest Group versus Current Freshmen on MSAT*

	N	M	S.D.
Retest group (45 years old)	634	56.2	11.9
1962 freshmen (tested as H.S. juniors at age 16)	3011	45.7	11.9

selectivity of the Williamson-Bordin group. Further, an inspection of the distributions suggests that this was an underestimate of the true difference since the MSAT did not have enough ceiling for the 25-year retest group. For example, although there are only 78 items on the MSAT, 2 percent of the group scored 75 or over. And although only 3 percent of the current freshmen scored above 70, 13 percent of the retest group did and they may well have scored higher, had they had the opportunity.

Clearly the older group scored much higher on today's scholastic aptitude test than current students do, although the retest group were close to average in their own class 25 years ago. The conclusion is inevitable that individuals who attend college are brighter, or at least score higher on scholastic aptitude tests, at age 45 than at age 16.

THE SCHOLASTIC ABILITIES GROWTH CURVE

This type of mental ability may mature at some earlier age and be waning or on some plateau by age 45. With only two points established on the curve, those at age 16 and 45, it is impossible to determine whether this ability is still rising, has leveled off, or is declining from some intervening peak.

Further data were collected to extend the MSAT growth curve to about age 20. In the fall of 1962, all students applying for advanced admission to the Arts College at Minnesota completed the Ohio State Psychological Examination No. 26, which has incorporated within it all the items of the MSAT. By comparing the student's performance as a high school junior with his performance on advanced admission, growth over this short period could be

TABLE 52. *MSAT Test-Retest Results over Varying Time Periods**

H.S. Gradua-tion Year	N	HSR		H.S. Jr. MSAT		1962 MSAT		Retest Interval (Months)	MSAT Growth
		M	S.D.	M	S.D.	M	S.D.		
1959+	42	69	20.4	42.8	12.7	56.2	11.5	54	13.4
1960+	225	74	22.3	45.4	14.2	57.0	11.9	42	11.6
1961+	313	75	21.0	46.4	13.1	55.9	11.8	30	9.5
1962*	383	75	18.4	44.8	11.9	52.2	12.1	18	7.4

*Random sample of entering freshmen.

+Students applying for advanced standing.

determined. Generally, these were students who had spent 1, 2 or 3 years at some other school, frequently their local junior college, before coming to the University. A random sample of 1962 entering freshmen also completed the Ohio No. 26. The results of that testing are presented in Table 52.

Because these groups were not comparable on HSR and initial MSAT scores, growth on the MSAT rather than final score is the more meaningful statistic. It is reported in the last column of Table 52. These figures, plotted against retest interval in months, indicate that the growth curve of these abilities followed a straight line during the college years for those students continuing on.

The magnitude of growth over the college years was slightly more than one standard deviation, a finding that closely agreed with the results of an earlier study by Laughlin at Minnesota (Laughlin, 1940). He retested 420 individuals after 3½ years of college with the Ohio State Psychological Examination No. 18 and found the average gain to be 1.2 standard deviation.

It should be noted here that the average growth found over 25 years in the retest group was also slightly more than one standard deviation. Thus, although these comparisons were confounded somewhat by the inadequate ceiling on the MSAT, it appears likely that most of the growth occurred during the college years.

A similar finding was reported by Owens in his study in which he retested 127 men 30 years after they had been tested as college freshmen (Owens, 1953). He found considerable gains and reported that these gains were probably achieved during the college years as opposed to later on in life.

Mental Growth and College Attendance

All of the data presented thus far were collected from college students, and it is not possible to determine if similar gains would be found in a non-collegiate population. Some knowledge can be generated on this point by comparing gain scores between groups with differing amounts of college study.

In Owens' study, he found that the groups with the most education showed the greatest gains. Swanson (1933), working only with individuals who were in the upper fifth of their high school class on grades and test scores, reported the same trend; the groups with the most education showed the greatest gain. His results seem particularly meaningful since the groups were initially roughly equal in ability.

The data from the current study also support this hypothesis of growth connected with college attendance.

TABLE 53. *Growth in Scholastic Abilities by Varying*
Educational Levels

Educational Level	N	1936 ACE M	1936 ACE S.D.	1962 MSAT M	1962 MSAT S.D.	ACE Mean Z Score	MSAT Mean Z Score	GAIN Mean Z Score
Less than 2 years	46	188.5	41.33	46.4	12.49	-0.43	-0.02	0.41
2-4 years	34	188.5	40.20	54.1	10.91	-0.42	.59	1.01
B.A.	82	216.5	50.91	59.2	10.37	0.17	.99	0.82
Graduate work	60	226.6	53.02	61.9	9.97	0.38	1.21	0.83

In Table 53, the retest group has been divided by educational level. The first category includes individuals with less than 2 years of college, the next category those with more than 2 years but less than a B.A., the third those with a 4-year degree only, and the last includes individuals with some graduate study or with professional degrees such as D.D.S., L.L.B., M.D., and all M.A.s and Ph.D.s. For these comparisons, only the individuals who had taken the 1936 ACE 25 years ago and the 1962 MSAT were used.

The first five columns in Table 53 show the number in each group and their scores on the two tests. The last three columns show the converted standard scores, and the gain between the two. (The mean and standard deviation of the 1962 freshmen group were used to establish these standard scores.)

The last column showing the gain from one test to the other is the pertinent one. These results show a mild trend toward more growth with more education, which might be even more pronounced were it not for the restrictive ceiling on the MSAT. The group with the most education, the graduate group, started highest on the earlier test but could not show much relative improvement on the MSAT, as their adult average, 62, was only one and one-half standard deviations below the highest possible score. Had they had the opportunity, they very likely would have demonstrated a larger increase. This conjecture was strengthened by the variability data on the two tests. On the 1936 ACE, the variability increased from group to group up the educational ladder, but on the MSAT the variability decreased, probably because some of the more intelligent individuals were held down by the ceiling.

Attention should be drawn to the size of the differences between these groups. On their 1936 ACE scores as entering freshmen, there was roughly three-fourths of a standard deviation difference (188 to 226) between those never graduating and those eventually doing graduate work. That difference in itself was large and significant, but the current difference on the MSAT, averaging about 1¼ standard deviations, was even more impressive (47 to 62). Clearly, although both of these groups have improved, the graduate group has gained more and the difference between them has widened.

These data, together with the work of Owens and Swanson, demonstrate that growth in these abilities is associated with college attendance, although they do not prove which is cause and which effect. Education may foster this increased growth or, alternatively, people who develop most may seek more education. From this study, it is impossible to tell which is happening, but some combination of factors would seem most plausible.

CORRELATIONS BETWEEN
TESTS AND GRADES OVER 25 YEARS

One other area explored in this chapter was the stability over several years of the relationship between various indices of academic ability, and the effect of time on the accuracy of prediction of these indices.

Correlations between various measures in two groups separated by 25 years are presented in Table 54. For example, the first row shows the correlation between high school rank and first quarter grade point average for the 1962 freshmen and for freshmen of the 30's. Obviously, the relationship between high school grades

TABLE 54. *Correlations between Various Measures in Freshmen Classes 25 Years Apart*

Variables	Classes	
	1962 Freshmen*	1933-1936 Freshmen†
GPA ‡ vs. HSR	.47	.52
GPA ‡ vs. 1936 ACE	.53	.52
GPA ‡ vs. 1933 CAT	.40	.33
HSR vs. 1936 ACE	.44	.37
HSR vs. 1933 CAT	.30	.14

* N = 476.

† N's vary from 262 to 601.

‡ First quarter only.

and college grades has remained stable. The other correlations in the table show the same trend.

Another indication of the stability of these measures is the comparison of correlations between measures collected at different points in time. These correlations are shown in Table 55, and again they indicate great stability. These figures show that the correlations between measures collected 25 years apart are virtually identical to correlations between those collected just 18 months apart.

TABLE 55.   *Correlations between Various Measures over Two Different Time Periods*

Variables	Time Lag Between Measures	
	18 Months*	25 Years†
	"r"	"r"
1st Qtr. GPA vs. MSAT	.51	.48
HSR vs. MSAT	.34	.34
1936 ACE vs. MSAT	.74	.70
1933 CAT vs. MSAT	.61	.51

*1962 freshmen, N = 476.

†1930's freshmen, N's vary from 214 to 602.

The stability of these correlations, coupled with the earlier figures showing growth of the individuals, leads to the conclusion that, although the group as a whole advanced upward, the rank order of individuals within the group remained fairly constant. This conclusion was strengthened by a scatter-chart showing the 25-year retest group scores of the 1930's against their scores now. High people stayed high; low people stayed low, although there were some substantial increases in individual cases. This point should probably be emphasized for the enlightenment of any administrators or institutions who make irreversible decisions on the basis of test scores alone. The quarter of the scatter chart showing cases "high then–low now" is virtually vacant. The quarter showing "low then–high now" has a healthy number of cases while, of course, the most populous quarters are those of "low then–low now" and "high then–high now."

One very disconcerting finding was the demonstration that there has been no progress in accuracy of grade point prediction since 1936. The correlation between the 1936 ACE and first quarter

GPA for 1936 freshmen was .52 and for 1962 freshmen, .53; the correlation between the MSAT, the University's 1962 entrance examination, and first quarter GPA for 1962 freshmen was .51. It is disturbing to note that at the University of Minnesota, an institution greatly interested in better student personnel administration, during the active years of extremely able people such as D. G. Paterson, E. G. Williamson, J. G. Darley, R. F. Berdie, and others of high capabilities, it has not been possible to increase even slightly the accuracy of student selection procedures. While there may be arguments that attempt to rationalize this lack of progress ("grades are not a truly important criterion," "we know much more about working with the individual student once he is here"), the cold, hard fact remains that superior or inferior students are no more accurately identified today by the University's admissions tests than they were 25 years ago. (It perhaps should be pointed out here that current scholastic aptitude tests are shorter, easier to administer, and less complicated to score than earlier versions. The same degree of accuracy is attained more simply now, but that is small consolation for lack of real improvement in accuracy.)

Apparently, the variance in college grades due to scholastic abilities has been adequately tapped. Motivation, study habits, personal involvement, a desire to achieve goals other than grades— these and other factors probably account for the remaining variance, and no psychological instrument available thus far measures these well. In a much earlier article, E. G. Williamson has pointed this out (Williamson, 1937). There has been little real progress; a breakthrough is needed.

CONCLUSIONS AND IMPLICATIONS

The results of the comparisons reported in this chapter support five main conclusions:

1. In scholastic abilities, the 1962 freshman class at the University of Minnesota was at least equal and possibly slightly superior to the freshmen classes of the mid-30's.

2. Individuals score far higher on scholastic aptitude tests at age 45 than at age 16.

3. Growth on scholastic ability tests is associated with length of college attendance.

4. The relationships between the various measures of academic ability and achievement, such as aptitude tests, high school grades, and college grades are very stable over long periods of time.

5. There has been no improvement in the accuracy of prediction of student performance over the last 25 years.

The implications of these conclusions seem both straightforward and, for the most part, reassuring. First, although many more people attend college today (the percentage of Minnesota students continuing on to college has roughly doubled during the past 25 years), the quality has not dropped, at least as measured by test performances. Whether this is due to a general improvement in the population or better selection of students is not clear; perhaps a combination of both factors is working. Whatever the reason, college faculties today have raw materials equal in quality to those of 25 years ago.

Second, although these data leave a considerable gap in the growth curve from the end of college to age 45, they do indicate that the average 45 year old does as well as the average college senior. Whether the 45 year old stopped improving at the end of college, or whether he is declining from some intervening peak is not clear.

Third, if we are willing to accept the assumption that the growth associated with college attendance was caused, at least to some extent, by that attendance, these results offer evidence of the value of education in fostering mental growth, and an empirical foundation for the assertion that one way of upgrading the populace is to educate them.

Last, is the disquieting conclusion that we have made no progress in the accuracy of grade-point prediction over the past 25 years. This surely qualifies as a plateau. As has proved true so often in other endeavors, any advance upward will require radically new approaches to the problem.

CHAPTER TWELVE

LIBERALS
AND CONSERVATIVES

Co-authored with Dr. Jack Rossmann,
Macalester College

Stereotypes of liberals and conservatives abound in popular literature; valid empirical descriptions of the two are more difficult to obtain. This chapter is an attempt to compare these two political types, using samples of college-educated citizens, on the various sociological and psychometric measures used in the earlier chapters.

In general, the approach used here was to ask the participants in the counseling follow-up study to sort themselves into political categories; then the differences between these categories were studied. Specifically, in the questionnaire, the individuals were asked to locate themselves on a 5-point scale of political liberalism-conservatism. Later, in the interview, they were asked which political party they usually agreed with most.

Using a combination of these two questions, the samples studied here were identified, i.e., Liberal Democrats and Conservative Republicans. Liberal Republicans, Conservative Democrats, and Independents—three groups totaling about 25 percent of the original group—were excluded. In the remaining group, the Conservative Republicans outnumbered the Liberal Democrats almost two to one. The numbers in each category are indicated in Table 56.

Differences between the two groups on a variety of variables, clustered together into meaningful groupings, are reported below.

TABLE 56. *Designation of the Criterion Groups*

	Very Conservative	Somewhat Conservative	Neither	Somewhat Liberal	Very Liberal
			Male		
Democrats	1	8	6	57	30
Republicans	36*	98	18	28	1
			Female		
Democrats	2	15	13	50	22
Republicans	30	120	22	28	--

*The boxed numbers indicate the categories included in this study.

Total male   N = 221   Total liberal   N = 159
Total female N = 222   Total conservative N = 284

Total N = 443

The first grouping, reported in Table 57, contains demographic information.

RELIGION

There were large and impressive differences in the religious preferences of the two groups. Substantially more of the conservatives reported Protestant affiliation, while the liberals more often were either Jewish or reported no preference. Roughly 10 percent of both groups were Catholic.

MARITAL STATUS

Significantly more of the conservatives were married and living with their original spouse. Thus, the liberals more often were single or had been widowed or divorced.

SOCIO-ECONOMIC LEVEL

Significantly more of the liberals had fathers who had not graduated from high school, while the conservatives more often

TABLE 57. *Liberals versus Conservatives on Sociological Variables*

Variable (in percent)	MEN Liberal N=91	MEN Conservative N=136	Level of Signif.	WOMEN Liberal N=72	WOMEN Conservative N=150	Level of Signif.	TOTAL Liberal N=163	TOTAL Conservative N=286	Level of Signif.
Religious preference									
Protestant	26.4	72.1	.001	36.1	75.3	.001	30.7	73.8	.001
Jewish	33.0	5.1	.001	26.4	1.3	.001	30.1	3.1	.001
Catholic	13.2	9.6	n.s.	11.1	12.0	n.s.	12.3	10.8	n.s.
None	17.6	9.6	n.s.	16.7	4.7	.01	17.1	7.0	.01
Other	9.8	3.6	n.s.	9.7	6.7	n.s.	9.8	5.3	n.s.
	100.0	100.0		100.0	100.0		100.0	100.0	
Marital status									
Married and living with original spouse	74.7	91.9	.001	70.8	77.3	n.s.	73.0	84.2	.01
Other	25.3	8.1		29.2	22.7		27.0	15.8	
	100.0	100.0		100.0	100.0		100.0	100.0	
Father's education									
Father did not graduate from high school	58.6	43.3	.05	47.3	30.6	.05	53.4	36.8	.001
Father graduated from high school but not from college	20.6	37.5	.05	30.5	41.9	n.s.	25.2	40.0	.01
Father a college graduate	20.6	19.1	n.s.	22.2	26.7	n.s.	21.4	23.2	n.s.
	99.8	99.9		100.0	99.2		100.0	100.0	

TABLE 58.   *Comparison of Political Liberals and Conservatives on Attitudes and Values*

Variable (In percent)	MEN			WOMEN			TOTAL		
	Liberal N=91	Conservative N=136	Level of Signif.	Liberal N=72	Conservative N=150	Level of Signif.	Liberal N=163	Conservative N=286	Level of Signif.
Favorable to modern art	36.3	19.9	.001	47.2	27.3	.01	41.1	23.8	.001
Conventional in opinions and values	41.8	74.3	.001	43.1	73.4	.001	42.4	73.7	.001
Religous	61.5	76.4	n.s.	59.7	84.0	.001	60.7	80.4	.001
Most proud of occupational accomplishments	65.5	50.8	.05	17.1	12.2	n.s.	43.9	30.4	.01
Most proud of family accomplishments	29.9	40.1	n.s.	54.3	66.2	n.s.	41.0	53.9	.05

had fathers who made it through high school but not college. There was no difference between the two groups in the percentage of fathers who were college graduates, about one-fifth of each group reporting that amount of education for their fathers.

ATTITUDES AND VALUES

One section of the questionnaire was concerned with the individual's value orientation as measured by his attitude toward modern art, conventionality in opinions and values, and degree of religiosity. Each individual was asked to place himself along a 5-point continuum dealing with each of the three areas. The choices ranged from very favorable toward modern art to very unfavorable. Analogous alternatives were presented for the other two variables. The data presented in Table 58 indicate the percentages falling in the favorable, conventional, and religious categories, respectively, for the three dimensions.

Two by five χ^2 tests indicated that all three variables were significantly related to political liberalism-conservatism. Whether both sexes were taken together or considered separately, liberals were found to be more favorable toward modern art, more unconventional in opinions and values, and less religious.

In a further attempt to determine what the individual thought was important, another interview question asked, "Which of your accomplishments are you most proud of?" Answers were coded into the following categories:

1. Occupation
2. Marriage
3. Family
4. Avocation
5. Education
6. Friends
7. Religiosity
8. Nothing
9. Other

The majority of the sample reported greatest pride in either their occupational or family accomplishments, although there was a surprising difference between the two groups as to which of those areas they selected. A substantially higher percentage of liberal males mentioned occupational success as the accomplishment of which they were most proud, while conservative males more frequently mentioned their family as the most satisfying aspect of their lives. The pattern, though not so dramatic and not statistically significant, was similar among the females.

TABLE 59. *Comparison of Political Liberals and Conservatives on Mental Health Variables*

Variables (In percent)	MEN		Level of	WOMEN		Level of	TOTAL		Level of
	Liberal N=91	Conservative N=136	Signif.	Liberal N=72	Conservative N=150	Signif.	Liberal N 163	Conservative N=286	Signif.
From questionnaire									
Has gone to psychiatrist or psychologist	24.4	9.6	.01	25.4	12.8	.05	24.8	11.2	.001
From interview									
Has gone to a professional person for help	34.9 (N=30)	22.0 (N=29)	n.s.	44.3 (N=31)	23.6 (N=35)	.01	39.1 (N=61)	22.8 (N=64)	.001
Psychiatrist or psychologist	70.0 (N=21)	48.3 (N=24)	n.s.	67.8 (N=21)	45.7 (N=16)	n.s.	68.8 (N=42)	46.9 (N=30)	.05
Minister or doctor	33.3 (N=10)	34.4 (N=10)	n.s.	25.8 (N=8)	59.9 (N=21)	.05	29.5 (N=18)	48.4 (N=31)	.05

MENTAL HEALTH

Several questions were asked of the participants in an attempt to ascertain their current emotional adjustment. On the questionnaire the subjects were asked whether they had ever gone to a psychiatrist or psychologist and, as reported in Table 59, a significantly higher percentage of liberals responded positively to the question.

In the interview, they were asked if they had ever gone to a professional person for help with any personal problems. Again, a significantly higher proportion of liberals said they had sought professional help. When asked the sources of this help, a greater percentage of the liberals said they had gone to a psychiatrist or psychologist, while those conservatives who had sought help were more likely to have gone to a minister or doctor.

The immediate conclusion to be drawn from these data is that the liberals have exhibited more personal instability than the conservatives, but this may be too hasty. A more extensive discussion by Schofield (1964) indicates that the number of persons seeking help from professional psychologists or psychiatrists is a poor gauge of the amount of mental illness in a population. Other factors, such as income and education, are more closely related to the individual's decision to seek help. Rather than demonstrating more personal instability, the liberal group may simply be more willing to utilize the services of professional people for emotional problems.

This issue has been discussed at greater length on page 67.

SCHOLASTIC APTITUDE AND ACHIEVEMENT

A distinction is drawn here—as is usually done in psychometric literature—between aptitude and achievement. Aptitude is presumably a more basic characteristic of the individual, less dependent on environmental experiences. Achievement, on the other hand, is more concerned with how well the individual has absorbed his education or training.

For an aptitude measure, the Minnesota Scholastic Ability Test (MSAT) was used. For measures of scholastic achievement, the following indices were available for each student:

1. High School Rank (HSR)—rank in the high school class, expressed in percentiles.
2. College Grade Point Average (GPA)—calculated on whatever college work the individual had completed at Minnesota, based on a 4-point scale with A = 4.00.
3. Percent graduating from college—includes all individuals earning a 4-year college degree at any institution.

TABLE 60. *Political Liberals versus Conservatives on Scholastic Ability and Achievement Variables*

Variable	MEN		Level of Signif.	WOMEN		Level of Signif.	TOTAL		Level of Signif.
	Liberal N=91	Conservative N=136		Liberal N=72	Conservative N=150		Liberal N=163	Conservative N=286	
Scholastic aptitude									
MSAT*									
Mean	57.5	58.3	n.s.	58.9	55.6	.05	58.1	56.9	n.s.
S.D.	13.4	10.0		11.5	11.8		12.5	11.1	
Scholastic achievement									
High School Rank									
Mean	71.9	70.2	n.s.	83.7	78.7	n.s.	77.2	74.6	n.s.
S.D.	22.4	22.4		19.9	18.1		20.7	21.4	
College GPA									
Mean	2.23	2.17	n.s.	2.50	2.11	.001	2.35	2.14	.01
S.D.	.78	.65		.74	.69		.77	.72	
Percent college graduates	70.3	65.2	n.s.	70.8	58.1	n.s.	70.5	61.2	.05
Percent graduate degrees	44.6	27.7	.01	17.8	3.9	.001	32.7	15.3	.001
Percent graduating with honors	12.8	5.8	n.s.	18.3	9.2	n.s.	15.1	7.6	.05
Percent on dean's list	10.6	2.9	.05	5.6	3.3	n.s.	8.5	3.1	.05
Percent in Phi Beta Kappa	5.3	1.4	n.s.	9.9	2.0	.05	7.3	1.7	.01

*MSAT Minnesota Scholastic Aptitude Test

4. Percent earning graduate honors—any degree beyond the B.A., e.g.,
   M.A., M.D., Ph.D.
5. Percent graduating with honors, i.e., Cum Laude, etc., based on subject's self-report.
6. Percent on dean's list for high scholastic achievement.
7. Percent earning Phi Beta Kappa recognition.

The data for the last three categories, and the degrees earned
at institutions other than Minnesota, were taken from the questionnaire.

The results of these comparisons between the two groups are
reported in Table 60.

There was little difference between the two groups on scholastic ability, although the difference between the two female
groups was statistically significant at the 5 percent level, favoring
the liberal group.

However, on the scholastic achievement measures, there was
a clear, consistent trend in favor of the liberals. The liberals performed better in high school, though not significantly so, earned
significantly better college grades, and 10 percent more of them
graduated from college as compared to the conservatives. Further-
more, over twice as many liberals received graduate degrees and
graduated with honors. Three times as many liberals as conservatives made the dean's list, and four times as many earned mem-
bership in Phi Beta Kappa, although the percentages in both of
these last two categories were small.

Although approximately equal in ability, the liberals consistently outperformed the conservatives in scholastic settings. It is,
of course, not clear whether there was any causal relationship
operating here, i.e., whether success in educational settings makes
one more liberal or vice versa.

ACHIEVEMENT SINCE COLLEGE

On the questionnaire, each individual was asked to complete
a check list of honors and awards earned since college. Although
the categories were broad, and it was left up to the individual to
decide what qualified as an award, differences still appeared between the two groups. Table 61 lists the categories of awards and
the difference between the groups.

The percentage listed for each category is the percentage
reporting something other than "none."

For the men, only two of the percentage differences were statistically significant, and none of the differences for the women
was significant. Nevertheless, an interesting pattern did emerge,
particularly among the men. The liberals were more likely to have

TABLE 61. *Percentage of Liberals and Conservatives Having Received Awards and Honors since Leaving College*

Award	Liberals	Conservatives	Difference	Chi-Square
Male	N=90	N=135		
Miscellaneous publications	15.6	3.0	+12.6	9.99*
Technical publications	32.2	20.0	+12.2	3.69
Other non-fiction publications	12.2	3.7	+ 8.5	4.71†
Patents	5.5	.7	+ 4.8	3.15
Fiction	4.4	.7	+ 3.7	1.92
Drama	3.3	.0	+ 3.3	2.38
Other awards	7.8	4.4	+ 3.4	.57
Art	3.3	.7	+ 2.6	.86
Civic awards	14.4	14.1	+ .3	.01
Invitational addresses	4.4	5.2	- .7	.004
Music	0.0	2.2	- 2.2	.69
Athletic	6.7	14.1	- 7.4	2.30
Armed Forces	13.3	21.5	- 8.1	1.89
Business	12.2	20.7	- 8.5	2.17

	Liberals	Conservatives	Difference	Chi-Square
Female	N=72	N=150		
Miscellaneous publications	11.1	4.0	+ 7.1	1.94
Other non-fiction publications	9.7	4.7	+ 5.0	1.34
Business awards	4.2	3.3	+ .9	.005
Invitational addresses	1.4	.7	+ .7	.05
Technical publications	4.2	4.0	+ .2	.09
Fiction	.0	.7	+ .7	.14
Drama	1.4	2.0	- .6	.04
Art	00.0	.7	- .7	.14
Music	0.0	.7	- .7	.14
Civic awards	6.9	8.7	- 1.8	.03
Athletic	2.8	6.7	- 3.9	.78
Other awards	6.9	14.7	- 7.8	2.04

*Significant at .01 level of confidence.
†Significant at .05 level of confidence

received awards for their writing activities while the conservatives received more awards in athletics, the military services and business activities. Again, in their accomplishments, the liberals were more oriented toward intellectual areas.

Another area of adult achievement is income. Each respondent was asked to report his total family income, including his (or her) spouse's income, income from investments, rental property, etc. The conservative men reported a median income of $16,000 and the Liberals $12,000, a difference significant at the 1 percent level. For the women, the difference was in the same direction but not statistically significant—conservative women reported a median family income of $14,000, liberals, $12,750. From a financial standpoint, the conservatives were clearly faring better than the Liberals.

In the work on counseling effectiveness, an attempt was made to rate each subject on his over-all contribution to society. (See page 83.) The results of comparing the two political types on this rating are reported in Table 62.

On this global rating of achievement, there were no differences between the liberals and conservatives. Though the earlier results

TABLE 62.   "Contribution to Society" Rating between Political
Liberals and Conservatives

| | MEN | | Level of | WOMEN | | Level of | TOTAL | | Level of |
	Liberal N=91	Conservative N=136	Signif.	Liberal N=72	Conservative N=150	Signif.	Liberal N=163	Conservative N=286	Signif.
Mean	10.36	10.50		10.90	10.41		10.61	10.45	
S.D.	1.86	1.92		2.07	2.33		2.26	1.87	
t-value	.57		n.s.	1.84		n.s.	.70		n.s.

indicated mildly different patterns of achievement between the two groups, both groups—based on this rating—have contributed equally when all varieties of accomplishments are considered.

Vocational Interests of
Liberals and Conservatives

As part of the counseling effectiveness study, most of the individuals in this research completed the Strong Vocational Interest Blank (SVIB) as adults in 1962. Scores of the liberals and conservatives were compared and differences larger than 4 points, all significant beyond the 1 percent level, are listed in Table 63. (The SVIB uses standard scores with a mean of 50 and standard deviation of 10.)

The themes running through the vocational interest differences are similar to the earlier findings. The liberals had more interests in common with the social service occupations, with the arts and sciences, and with men and women in verbal-linguistic occupations. The conservative men tended toward business activities and the more practical, typically masculine occupations, while the conservative women showed greatest similarity in interests with the more domestic, typically feminine occupations. In both sexes, the conservatives leaned toward the practical, down-to-earth, traditional interests while the liberals indicated more interest in artistic, cultural, and intellectual areas and in service toward others.

The analysis of the vocational interests of these samples was extended one step further; the responses of the liberals and conservatives to the items of the SVIB were tabulated to identify those items in which the groups responded differently and these particular items were then collected into a liberalism-conservatism scale. Separate scales were prepared for both the men and women's form.

Specifically, items were included on the scales when at least one of the three possible response positions (like–indifferent–dislike) showed a 17 percent or greater response frequency between the two criterion groups. (On the men's form, the item selection was restricted to the 298 items being retained in the 1965 revision of the SVIB; on the women's blank, all 400 items were used.) Forty-seven items met this standard for the men's blank, 54 for the women's. The decision to select items in this manner was based on the work of Clark (1961). He has shown that scales with such characteristics are valid, reliable and hold up well under cross-validation.

Because these methods have been resistant to cross-validation

TABLE 63. *SVIB Scale Differences between Liberals and Conservatives*

Scale	Liberal Mean	Conservative Mean	Difference
Men	N=87	N=134	
Psychologist	35.9	24.1	11.8*
Musician	38.1	27.0	11.1*
Social worker	39.2	29.6	9.6*
Minister	27.6	18.8	8.8*
Artist	26.9	19.2	7.7*
City school superintendent	32.5	25.1	7.4*
Lawyer	38.2	31.3	6.9*
Author-journalist	35.6	28.7	6.9*
Social science HS teacher	37.4	30.7	6.7*
Physician	33.9	27.9	6.0*
Advertising man	37.4	31.6	5.8*
Mathematician	23.2	17.8	5.4*
Architect	27.0	21.6	5.4*
Farmer	26.0	29.9	-3.9*
Banker	26.5	30.5	-4.0*
President, mfg. concern	29.8	33.8	-4.0*
Engineer	24.1	28.1	-4.0†
Sales manager	31.0	35.1	-4.1†
Forest service man	18.9	23.1	-4.2†
Aviator	25.8	30.1	-4.3†
Office man	31.8	36.6	-4.8*
Production manager	28.7	35.4	-6.7*
Accountant	26.3	33.1	-6.8*
Purchasing agent	25.5	34.1	-8.6*
Women	N=72	N=149	
Psychologist	34.8	24.6	10.2*
English teacher	33.2	25.3	7.9*
Lawyer	34.0	27.2	6.8*
Social worker	38.3	31.7	6.6*
Author	34.3	28.1	6.2*
Social science teacher	30.1	24.3	5.8*
Librarian	35.4	30.4	5.0*
Elementary teacher	29.0	33.6	-4.6*
Nurse	24.5	29.4	-4.9*
Steno-secretary	31.5	36.6	-5.1*
Housewife	33.4	38.9	-5.5*
Office worker	30.8	37.0	-6.2*
Buyer	18.9	25.6	-6.7*
Dietitian	22.1	30.5	-8.4*
Home economics teacher	17.6	27.2	-9.6*

*Significant at .01 level of confidence.
†Significant at .05 level of confidence.

shrinkage, no attempt was made to directly cross-validate these scales; rather, all available subjects were used in the validation groups to increase the stability of the item selection procedures.

However, considerable validity generalization data have been collected. First, a group of current college freshmen, separated into the same two political criterion categories as used in the validation samples, were studied, and, second, all of the SVIB occupational criterion groups were scored on these scales. The distributions of occupational group means provided considerable information about the scale characteristics.

VALIDITY RESULTS

The results from scoring the validation groups are reported in Table 64. Since the items were weighted +1 when the liberal group answered more frequently, and −1 when the difference favored the conservatives, positive raw scores are in the liberal direction, negative raw scores in the conservative direction.

TABLE 64. *Validities of the Liberalism-Conservatism Scales*

		Men			Women	
Criterion Groups	N	Mean	S.D.	N	Mean	S.D.
Liberals	87	60.0	11.9	69	58.8	10.7
		(5.7)*	(8.6)		(11.4)	(13.4)
Conservatives	134	40.0	9.1	149	40.2	9.3
		(-8.8)	(6.6)		(-12.1)	(11.7)
		34			33	
			Percent Overlap			
Sub Groups	N	Mean	S.D.	N	Mean	S.D.
Very liberal	30	64.3	11.6	21	62.0	9.8
Somewhat liberal	57	57.7	11.4	48	57.4	10.7
Somewhat conservative	98	39.9	9.1	120	41.2	9.3
Very conservative	36	40.4	8.8	29	35.8	8.2

*Numbers in parentheses are raw scores; all others in standard score form.

When scores are reported for the usual SVIB occupational scales, they are transferred into standard scores with a mean of 50 and a standard deviation of 10. A slight modification has been used with the liberalism-conservatism scales. By applying the following conversion to the raw scores, they have been transformed into a distribution in which the conservatives average approximately 40, the liberals approximately 60, with a within-group standard deviation roughly equal to 10.

$$\text{L-C Standard Score} = \left[\frac{X - \left[\dfrac{M_L + M_C}{2} \right]}{\dfrac{SD_L + SD_C}{2}} \right] 10 + 50$$

Where X   = Subject's raw score
        M_L = Liberal mean
        M_C = Conservative mean
       SD_L = Liberal standard deviation
       SD_C = Conservative standard deviation

For the men's scale, $(M_L + M_C)/2 = -1.55$, and $(SD_L + SD_C)/2 = 7.6$. For the women's scale, the analogous figures are -0.33 and 12.58.

This transformation provides a ready reference to the scores of the original liberal and conservative criterion groups.

The most important figures in Table 64 are those showing the percent overlap between the two contrasting groups. This statistic, suggested by Tilton (1938), gives an indication of how many scores in one distribution can be matched by scores in the other. Complete separation would be indicated by zero overlap; complete similarity would show 100 percent overlap. The percent overlap is roughly twice the numbers of classification errors that would be made if the individual were assigned to one of the groups on the basis of his score on this scale, assuming the groups were equal in size and variability.

For the men, the overlap was 34 percent. For the women, the figure was 33 percent. These validity indices are of the same general magnitude as those for the regular SVIB occupational scales, and indicate that the L-C scales did a respectable job of separating the groups.

In the bottom half of Table 64, the liberal criterion groups have been split according to whether the subjects described themselves as "very liberal" or only "somewhat liberal." An analogous split has been made in the conservative groups. If the scales are operating as they should, the means should march in the desired direction within each sex. As the data indicate, with the exception of the male conservative group, the means march; the scales were sensitive to this discrimination.

As discussed earlier, all of the available subjects were used in the validation groups and no cross-validation sample was studied. While the progression of the sub-group means in Table 64 provides some assurance that the differences are not based on chance, more substantial evidence was gathered through the study of other samples.

The first included men who entered Macalester College as freshmen in the fall of 1964. During their college orientation, they filled out the SVIB and a questionnaire which included both the 5-point scale of liberalism and conservatism and the question on political party preference. The same two categories used in the developmental samples were separated out and scored on the L-C scale. The N, mean, and standard deviation for each group, and overlap between the groups are reported in Table 65.

TABLE 65. *Average Scores for Macalester College Freshmen Males*

	N	M	S.D.
Liberal Democrats	61	56.0	11.9
Conservative Republicans	81	49.1	9.1

Percent overlap: 74

While the difference between groups was safely beyond the chance level (t = 3.79, p<.001), the magnitude of the separation was considerably less than among the adult criterion groups. Some of the decrease may have been caused by cross-validation shrinkage, but probably more was due to the nature of the sample. These students, about 18 years old, probably had less well-defined political attitudes and certainly, from what is known about the age of onset of stability in interests, had less stable vocational interests than the adult samples.

A second type of validity generalization data was gathered by scoring each of the SVIB occupational criterion groups on the L-C scales. These groups, which ranged in size from 113 to 1024 with a median of about 300, contained the individuals originally used to standardize the SVIB scales. The male groups are ordered, according to their means, in the left hand column of Table 66; the women's groups are ordered in the right-hand column. As can be seen, there were substantial differences between the group means, almost two standard deviations between the extremes.

For the most part, the ordering corresponded to the usual expectations. For the men's groups, the occupations toward the conservative end were mainly those from the business world. Policemen and Army officers were also rated conservative by this scale, as were farmers and veterinarians. These four groups all have a certain

TABLE 66. *Occupational Mean Scores on the L-C Scales*

M	Men Occupations	M	Women Occupations
59	Author-journalist (248, 8.9)* Librarian (425, 10.4)	59	
58		58	
57	Social worker (400, 10.9)	57	Author (385, 7.5)
56	Psychologist (1045, 9.7)	56	
55		55	Psychologist (378, 8.8)
54	Artist (231, 8.3); Minister (250, 9.3)	54	
53	Music teacher (493, 10.6) Psychiatrist (404, 10.4)	53	
52	Mathematician (181, 8.1) Musician (450, 10.6)	52	Artist (385, 8.1) Librarian (417, 8.5)
51	Biologist (342, 9.8) Rehabilitation counselor (272, 10.7) Social science teacher (217, 10.2)	51	Social worker (464, 9.6) Physician (413, 8.6) Lawyer (369, 8.8)
50	Advertising man (169, 10.2) Lawyer (251, 10.1) School superintendent (190, 9.7)	50	English teacher (291, 8.4)
49	Architect (240, 9.2)	49	
48	CPA owner (354, 10.3) Physicist (172, 8.0) YMCA secretary (113, 9.1)	48	Social science teacher (392, 9.2)
47	Chamber of Commerce exec. (400, 10.0) Public administrator (550, 11.9)	47	Life insurance saleswoman (200, 8.0) Engineer (322, 9.3) YWCA secretary (197, 8.8) Musician (287, 9.6)
46	Physician (534, 10.4) Business teacher (323, 10.3)	46	Dentist (187, 9.0)
45	Math-science teacher (289, 8.8) Personnel director (147, 10.5) Printer (270, 9.9)	45	
44	Physical therapist (350, 9.5) YMCA physical director (216, 8.5) Life insurance salesman (310, 9.0)	44	Physical therapist (449, 9.0) Music teacher (444, 8.8) Math-science teacher (466, 8.5)
43	Chemist (297, 9.6) Pharmacist (309, 9.9) Real estate salesman (243, 9.4)	43	Laboratory technician (350, 8.4) Nurse (386, 8.8) Occupational therapist (162, 8.3)
42	Dentist (239, 8.4) Forest service man (406, 8.3) Osteopath (585, 9.0) Senior CPA (612, 9.4)	42	Buyer (196, 9.0) Steno-secretary (447, 8.7)
41	Accountant (345, 9.7) Mortician (360, 9.4) President, mfg. concern (169, 9.1) Sales manager (228, 9.1) Office worker (326, 8.9)	41	
40	Army officer (463, 9.2) Banker (247, 9.0) Credit manager (452, 9.5) Engineer (513, 8.4)	40	Business education teacher (250, 7.8) Physical education teacher (101, 6.5) Dietitian (415, 8.4)

*First number in parentheses is Group N; second number is group S.D.

Table 66 (Cont'd). *Occupational Mean Scores on the L-C Scales*

M	Men Occupations	M	Women Occupations
39	Farmer (241, 9.0) Policeman (254, 7.5) Production manager (216, 8.3)	39	Office worker (423, 7.8)
38	Carpenter (181, 7.5) Purchasing agent (219, 8.4) Veterinarian (310, 7.8)	38	Home economics teachers (417, 7.6)
37	Airplane pilot (510, 8.1)	37	

rugged, masculine flair and they share, with businessmen, common interests in things practical versus things intellectual, in the concrete versus the abstract.

On the liberal end of the men's scale were the intellectual and linguistic occupations. The arts and social welfare occupations were represented there also. The ordering makes it clear that the liberal end of the scale represented the intellectual portion of the Democratic party, not the labor bloc. On this scale, the 181 men in the carpenter group, an occupation traditionally oriented toward the Democratic party, had an average score far to the conservative end of the table. This result probably occurred because the Democrats used in this study were mostly college graduates; there were very few blue-collar workers represented.

Among the women's groups, those at the conservative end were in the occupations most closely concerned with "traditional domestic" activities, i.e., home economics teachers and dietitians, and also the business groups, such as buyers and business education teachers. Women physical education teachers, perhaps the closest analogy to the "rugged, masculine" occupations found at the conservative end of the men's scale, were also rated conservative by the women's scale.

The most liberal women's occupations were the authors, psychologists, social workers, and librarians, precisely the same as among the men's groups.

The variability within each of these occupations should be emphasized. The numbers in parenthesis in Table 66 include the standard deviation within each group. They averaged about 10, indicating that the men or women within each occupation were distributed over 50 or 60 points. The diversity within occupations is obvious and should be stressed.

RELIABILITY

The reliability of the men's scale was estimated by the use of two test-retest groups, the first with a 30-day interval, the second with a 22-year interval between testings. The first group included 102 individuals, most of whom were members of an Army Reserve unit, based at Fort Snelling, Minnesota. These men were roughly 25 years old, predominantly college-educated, and scattered across a variety of occupations, although there was a fair concentration in the advertising and newspaper fields.

The second test-retest group included 199 former Stanford University students studied by E. K. Strong, Jr. (1955) over a 22-year interval, beginning when they were college seniors.

The reliabilities, means, and standard deviations for each group are reported in the next table. Note that both groups had mean scores approximately in the middle of the scale.

TABLE 67.   *Test-Retest Reliability—Men's Scale*

Test-Retest Interval	N	Test		Retest		r t-r
		M	S.D.	M	S.D.	
30 Day	102	52.1	11.7	51.2	12.1	.91
22 Year	199	50.1	9.5	47.9	11.0	.64

The scale showed respectable stability with test-retest correlations of .91 over 30 days and .64 over 22 years.

The means for the 30-day retest group remained stable, but the 22-year group moved toward the conservative end of the scale. Though the change was not great, about one-fifth of a standard deviation, it was enough to be statistically significant. These Stanford University graduates were slightly more conservative as adults than they had been as college seniors.

No test-retest data are available on the women's scale.

ITEM CONTENT

Inspection of the item content of empirically derived scales can be risky since it frequently leads to over-interpretation; it also can provide tentative explanations as to why the scales work and can lead to hypotheses for further study.

In item preferences, the male liberals tended toward the "arty" and intellectual items, the conservatives toward the practical, business, and adventuresome activities. The business versus culture pattern appeared in the occupational titles, among which the conservatives more often reported liking for "building contractor," "factory manager," "manufacturer," "stock broker," and "wholesaler." Conversely, the liberals more often stated preferences for "poet," "newspaper reporter," and "sculptor."

The conservative's well-known concern for fiscal responsibility was reflected in other items showing differences between the groups. More often than the liberals, conservatives liked "thrifty people," "saving money," "being treasurer of a club," "people who have made fortunes in business," and reported that they were less apt to loan money to acquaintances.

The "intellectual versus practical" pattern was again reflected in the magazine preferences of the two groups, the liberals more often preferring the *New Republic* and *Atlantic Monthly,* the conservatives choosing *Popular Mechanics.* However, both groups reported greater preference for *Time* and the *National Geographic* than for any of the others.

This is perhaps an appropriate place to emphasize the similarity in interests of these two groups. People have more interests in common than they do differences (E. K. Strong, Jr. has pointed this out many times), and it was again established in this project. Of the several hundred items on the SVIB, large and substantial differences were found on only about 10 percent of the items. While it is these differences in interests that lead people to choose different occupations and different ways of life (and interest inventories capitalize on these differences), the phenomenon of substantial communality of interests over all groups should not be overlooked.

It should also be emphasized here that these scales represent *differences* between the liberal and conservative groups, not *absolute likes and dislikes.* For example, the response "like to be an explorer" was scored in the conservative direction; yet a majority of the liberal men (51 percent) responded that way. It was scored in the conservative direction because substantially more conservatives (73 percent) said they would like this occupation.

The differences in item responses between the women's groups indicated that liberal women, like the men, were more likely to have interests along verbal and intellectual lines. Whereas among the conservatives the men tended toward practical or business activities, the women reported interests typical of the traditional feminine, homemaking role.

The cultural versus homemaking dichotomy was well demonstrated by differences in occupational and amusement preferences. Liberal women more often liked the occupations of "dramatist," "editor" and "poet," while the conservatives more often chose "florist," "hostess," and "tea room proprietor."

In the area of amusements, the liberal women more often expressed preference for the magazines *Atlantic Monthly* and *New Republic,* while the conservatives preferred "women's pages," "romantic stories," "afternoon teas" and the magazines *National Geographic* and *Reader's Digest.*

Personality and Occupation

This liberalism-conservatism scale demonstrates the close relationship between the individual's location on this dimension and the way he has chosen to spend the majority of his waking hours, i.e., at work. Of course, there were wide differences within each sample, and it is by no means possible to predict accurately an individual's occupation from his score on the L-C scale, or vice versa; however, a substantial relationship clearly exists.

The identification of such a dimension among a set of interest inventory items also provides considerable information about the stability of such attitudes. It has been well-established that the SVIB scale results are remarkably stable over periods as long as 30 years (Strong, 1955; Campbell, 1965), and the liberalism-conservatism scale also has proved fairly reliable, with a test-retest correlation of .64 over a 22-year period. From all we know about the crystallization of interests, the individual's responses to the items on the L-C scale, and presumably his corresponding attitudes, will not vary much after about age 25.

LIBERALS AND CONSERVATIVES: A SUMMING UP

A variety of sociological and psychometric factors emerged as related to self-defined liberalism-conservatism. In summary fashion, the liberal, as contrasted with the conservative, could be characterized as being more likely to:

1. Be non-Protestant and less religious.
2. Have a father who did not graduate from high school.
3. State he is favorable toward modern art.
4. State he is unconventional in opinions and values.
5. Be proud of his occupational accomplishments.
6. Have gone to a psychiatrist or psychologist.
7. Have been a better student in college.
8. Have published more of his writing and have common interests with people in artistic, verbal, or social service occupations.

In contrast, the conservative is more likely to:

1. Be Protestant and fairly religious.
2. Have a stable marriage.
3. Express pride in his family rather than his occupational achievements.
4. Report that he is conventional in attitudes and opinions.
5. State distaste for modern art.

6. Have made contributions in the civic, business, or military areas; and have common interests with individuals in business or "masculine-oriented" occupations.

The nature and magnitude of these differences permits wide latitude in interpretation. One might say that the overwhelming finding is that of only small and, for the most part, trivial differences between these groups. On the really important variables of basic ability and general achievement, the groups are identical. This approach would probably appeal to at least one great American. George Washington, in his Farewell Address, 1796, pointed out the dangers of seeing political differences where none exist and stressed that the goals of the leading political parties in America have more in common than in conflict:

> The common and continual mischiefs of the spirit of Party are sufficient to make it the interest and duty of a wise People to discourage and restrain it. . . . It is certain there will always be enough of that spirit for every salutary purpose, and there being constant danger of excess, the effort ought to be, by force of public opinion, to mitigate and assuage it. A fire not to be quenched; it demands a uniform vigilance to prevent its bursting into a flame, lest, instead of warming, it should consume.

On the other hand, one could point out that despite the superficial nature of much of this information, despite the categorization based on only self-report, and despite the homogeneous distributions of the groups on variables such as geographic and ethnic origin, age, and educational background, consistent, meaningful, differences persisted across several varieties of data, all indicating the same basic dichotomy: a traditional, practical, business, or domestic orientation versus an intellectual, cultural, social service viewpoint.

I do not care to make either too much or too little of this difference. It is there, it exists and, as a matter of fact, to some of the people involved, it is a highly significant fact in their way of life. A few individuals on both extremes, the illiberal liberals and the radical conservatives, expressed concern informally in the interview that the other end was taking us straight into an authoritarian state, Communistic as seen from one end, Fascistic from the other.

But, with the possible exceptions of the extremes, considerable overlap was noted on all variables. While we need to attend to the differences to understand these two political types, we should not ignore the equally important phenomenon of substantial similarity.

BIBLIOGRAPHY

Aldrich, M. G.: An exploratory study of social guidance at the college level. *Educ. Psychol. Measmt.*, 2:209–216, 1942.

Aldrich, M. G.: A follow-up study of social guidance at the college level. *J. Appl. Psychol.*, 33:258–264, 1949.

Baller, W. R.: Characteristics of college students who demonstrate interest in counseling services, *J. Educ. Psychol.*, 35:302–308, 1944.

Berdie, R. F.: Changes in self-ratings as a method of evaluating counseling. *J. Couns. Psychol.*, 1:49–54, 1954.

Berdie, R. F., and Hood, A. B.: Trends in post-high school plans over an 11-year period. Cooperative Research Project No. 951, University of Minnesota, 1963.

Campbell, D. P.: A cross-sectional and longitudinal study of scholastic abilities over twenty-five years. *J. Couns. Psychol.*, 12:55–61, 1965.

Campbell, D. P.: The stability of interests within an occupation over 30 years. *J. Appl. Psychol.* (in press).

Cantoni, L. J.: Long-term effects of the Flint, Michigan, guidance experiment. *Psychol. Rep.*, 1:359–362, 1955.

Clark, K. E.: *Vocational Interests of Nonprofessional Men*. Minneapolis, University of Minnesota Press, 1964.

Cole, R. C.: Evaluating a boys' club guidance program. *Occupations*, 17:705–708, 1939.

Faries, M.: Short-term counseling at the college level. *J. Couns. Psychol.*, 2:182–184, 1955.

Golburgh, S. J., and Glanz, E. C.: Group counseling with students unable to speak in class. *J. Coll. Stud. Pers.*, 4:102–104, 1962.

Gray, J.: *The University of Minnesota 1851–1951*. Minneapolis, University of Minnesota Press, 1951.

Guthrie, G. M., and O'Neill, H. W.: Effects of dormitory counseling on academic achievement. *Pers. Guid. J.*, 31:307–309, 1953.

Hills, D. A., and Williams, J. E.: Effects of test information upon self evaluation in brief educational-vocational counseling. *J. Couns. Psychol.* (in press).

Hoppock, R.: *Job Satisfaction*. New York, Harper & Brothers, 1935.

Hoyt, D. P.: Differential outcomes of counseling with college men. Unpublished doctoral dissertation, University of Minnesota, 1954.

Ivey, A. E.: The academic performance of students counseled at a university counseling service. *J. Couns. Psychol.*, 9:347–352, 1962.

Jesness, C. F.: The effects of counseling on the self-perceptions of college men. *Diss. Abstr.*, 15:1553, 1955.

Kilpatrick, F. P., and Cantril, H.: Self-anchoring scaling: a measure of individuals' unique reality world. *J. Ind. Psychol.*, 16:158–173, 1960.

Kirchheimer, B. A., et al.: An objective evaluation of counseling. *J. Appl. Psychol.*, 33:249–257, 1949.

Lorimer, M.: An appraisal of vocational guidance. *J. Higher Educ.*, 15:260–267, 1944.

Magoon, T. M.: General and specific outcomes of counseling with college men. Unpublished doctoral dissertation, University of Minnesota, 1954.

Martinson, W. D.: Utilization of the role construct reportory test in the counseling process. *Diss. Abstr.*, 15:2102–2103, 1955.

Porter, E. H.: Clients' evaluation of services at the University of Chicago counseling center. *J. Couns. Psychol.*, 4:274–282, 1957.

Rothney, J. W. M.: *Guidance Practices and Results.* New York, Harper & Brothers, 1958.

Scarborough, B. B., and Wright, J. C.: The assessment of an educational guidance clinic. *J. Couns. Psychol.*, 4:283–286, 1957.

Schachter, S.: *The Psychology of Affiliation.* Stanford University Press, 1959.

Schneidler, G. G. and Berdie, R. F.: Representativeness of college students who receive counseling services. *J. Educ. Psychol.*, 33:545–551, 1942.

Schofield, W.: *Psychotherapy: the Purchase of Friendship.* Englewood Cliffs, New Jersey, Prentice-Hall, Inc., 1964.

Sherriffs, A. C.: Modification of academic performance through personal interview. *J. Appl. Psychol.*, 33, 339–351, 1949.

Spielberger, C. D., Weitz, H., and Denny, J. P.: Group counseling and the academic performance of anxious college freshmen. *J. Couns. Psychol.*, 9:195–204, 1962.

Stone, C. H., and Simos, I.: A follow-up study of personal counseling versus counseling by letters. *J. Appl. Psychol.*, 32:408–414, 1948.

Strong, E. K., Jr.: *Vocational interests 18 years after college.* Minneapolis, University of Minnesota Press, 1955.

Tilton, J. W.: The measurement of overlapping. *J. Educ. Psychol.*, 45:656–662, 1938.

Viteles, M. S.: Validating the clinical method in vocational guidance. *Psychol. Clin.*, 18:69–77, 1929.

Volsky, T., Jr., Magoon, T. M., Norman, W. T., and Hoyt, D. P.: *The outcomes of counseling and psychotherapy.* Minneapolis, University of Minnesota Press, 1965.

Vosbeck, P. D.: An exploratory study of the effects of counseling. Master's Thesis, 1959.

Ward, J. R.: An evaluation of the veterans administration counseling program at the University's of Oregon. Unpublished Master's Thesis, University of Oregon, 1948.

Watson, G. H.: An evaluation of counseling with college students. *J. Couns. Psychol.*, 8:99–104, 1961.

White, L.: The measurement of occupational satisfaction. Unpublished mimeographed report. Minneapolis, Student Counseling Bureau, University of Minnesota, 1962.

Williams, J. E.: Changes in self and other perceptions following brief educational-vocational counseling. *J. Couns. Psychol.*, 9:18–30, 1962.

Williams, J. E., and Hills, D. A.: More on brief educational-vocational counseling. *J. Couns. Psychol.*, 9:366–368, 1962.

Williamson, E. G.: *Student Personnel Services in College and Universities; Some Foundations, Techniques, and Processes of Program Administration.* New York, McGraw-Hill Book Co., Inc., 1961.

Williamson, E. G., and Bordin, E. S.: Evaluating counseling by means of a control-group experiment. *School & Society*, 52:434–440, 1940. Also in Brayfield, A. H. (ed): *Readings in Modern Methods of Counseling.* New York, Appleton-Century-Crofts, Inc., 1950, pp. 511–520.

Williamson, E. G., and Darley, J. G.: *Student Personnel Work.* New York, McGraw-Hill Book Co., Inc., 1937.

Worbois, G. M.: Effect of guidance program on emotional development. *J. Appl. Psychol.*, 31:169–181, 1947.

APPENDIX

APPENDIX I is the questionnaire sent to each participant in the 25-year follow-up study. It was returned to the University when it had been completed.

APPENDIX II is the guidance form used by the interviewers who made personal contact with the study participants.

APPENDIX I

UNIVERSITY OF MINNESOTA RESEARCH QUESTIONNAIRE

(Men's Form)

In the following pages we are asking you for detailed information about yourself. Some questions pertain to your current status and some are historical in nature. Usually you can answer the questions with a simple check mark or short phrase. In this way we can obtain the bulk of the information we need and minimize the imposition on your time.

We realize the shortcomings of this "check-mark" system. Life is not simple, and many times cannot be cut up neatly into a list of categories. In those instances where no categories accurately represent your situation, **mark the best answer available**, and then qualify your response in the margin. We will make use of these notes in our use of the data.

We hope that you will not omit any of the information requested.

Please fill in the following blanks on this cover sheet. DO NOT PUT YOUR NAME ANYWHERE ELSE ON THE QUESTIONNAIRE. When you return the completed form, this cover sheet will be removed and a code number given to the remaining pages of the questionnaire. In this way, no one but the project directors will have any knowledge of whose questionnaire it is. All reports of   data will be in summary form to assure anonymity for each individual.

THE UTMOST CONFIDENCE WILL BE MAINTAINED

NAME _____

     First   Middle   Last

WIFE'S NAME _____

      First   Middle   Maiden

David P. Campbell
Theo. Volsky

149

Leave this
column blank

* * * * * * * * * * * *

Code No. _____

PERSONAL DATA

1-3

* * * * * * * * * * * *

[___]
10

1. AGE _____(at last birthday)

[___]
11

2. CURRENT MARITAL STATUS

[___]
12

A.   _____ Single (never married)   _____ Widowed

_____ Married   _____ Separated

_____ Divorced   _____ Other (specify)

_____

B.   If you have been married more than once, what terminated your previous
marriage/s; (e.g. divorce, widowed, etc.)

[___]
13

_____

C.   Number of children _____

[___]
14

Number of grandchildren _____

[___]
15

* * * * * * * * * * * *

EDUCATION

* * * * * * * * * * * *

3.	COLLEGE	MAJOR	NUMBER OF YEARS ATTENDED	DEGREE(s) AND YEAR OBTAINED	
	UNIVERSITY OF MINNESOTA				[___] 16
					[___] 17
					[___] 18

Leave this
Column blank

3.

A.   IF YOU DID NOT GRADUATE, please check the following statements
      which are applicable and CIRCLE THE ONE WHICH IS THE MOST
      IMPORTANT.

_____ Dropped out because I was uncertain about my goals.
_____ Was not interested in school work.
_____ Wanted to go to work right away.
_____ Did not have the ability.
_____ Got married, or planned to marry shortly.   [___]
_____ Was needed at home.   19
_____ It seemed financially impossible to continue.
_____ Parents did not encourage my continuing.
_____ Personal illness.
_____ Decided to go to technical, business, or proprietary school.
_____ Entered the service.
_____ Other (specify) _____

      _____

4.   To your best recollection, what was your chief means of support
      in college. (Please check applicable sources and fill in
      percentages.)   APPROX. PERCENTAGE

_____ Parental support (including loans)   _____
_____ Self-employment   _____
_____ Savings   _____   [___]
_____ Other loans   _____   20
_____ Working wife   _____
_____ Scholarship   _____
_____ Other (specify below)   _____

      _____   100 % = Total

****

COLLEGE EXTRA-CURRICULAR ACTIVITIES

****

5.   In which of the following were you an active participant during
      college. (Check any which apply.)

_____ Off-campus organizations.
_____ Editorial staff of campus publication.
_____ Musical or dramatic group.
_____ Business staff of campus publication or other campus group.   [___]
_____ Campus group concerned with national or world issues.   21
_____ Inter-collegiate (varsity) athletics.
_____ Fraternity, or equivalent.
_____ Special interest group; (e.g., Psychology Club, Rover's Club.)
_____ Student government.
_____ YMCA, other religious groups.
_____ Other (Check and specify)_____

Leave this
column blank

6.   Did you hold any elected student offices when you were in
college.

_____ NO   _____ YES   If YES, how many? _____   [___]
                                                                           22

7.   About how much time per week would you say you spent on extra-
curricular activities.

_____ Less than 1 hour.   _____ 2-4 hours.   _____ 11-20 hours.
_____ 1 hour   _____ 5-10 hours.   _____ Over 20 hours.   [___]
                                                                           23

8.   Do you feel any of the above activities contributed something of
considerable value to your life during college.

_____ NO   _____ YES   If YES, which ones? _____
                           _____   [___]
                                                                           24

9.   Looking back from 25 years perspective, do you feel that any of
them were a waste of time.

_____ NO   _____ YES   If YES, which ones? _____
                           _____   [___]
                                                                           25

10.   Do you now feel these activities were valuable for post-college
life.

_____ NO   _____ YES   If YES, which ones? _____
                           _____   [___]
                                                                           26

11.   Do you think students should be as involved with extra-curricular
activities as you were.

More involved _____   As involved_____   Less involved_____   [___]
                                                                           27

12.   Listed below are a number of awards and honors. Which of these
did you receive during college. (Check any which apply.)

_____ Dean's list (for high scholarship)
_____ Phi Beta Kappa
_____ Other honor society based on academic achievement
_____ Graduation with honors (Cum, Magna, Summa)
_____ Honor society based on leadership
_____ Other scholarship awarded on the basis of academic ability
_____ Participation in "honors program" at this school   [___]
_____ Prize or award for scholarship or research work; (e.g., "Smith   28
                         prize for best biology experiment")
_____ Prize or award for literary, musical, or artistic work
_____ Took one or more graduate-level courses as an undergraduate
_____ Other award or honor (Check and specify) _____
      _____

Leave this
column blank

13.   Please call to mind the students who were your closest male
        friends during college. Where did you meet them.
        (Check any which apply.)

        ____ Knew them before I came here.   ____ Classes in my major field.
        ____ Dormitory or rooming house.   ____ Classes in other fields.   [____]
        ____ My fraternity or equivalent.   ____ Other (Check and specify)   29
        ____ Campus activities.   _____

                            ____ No close friends at college.

****

GENERAL QUESTIONS REGARDING COLLEGE DAYS

****

14.   Which of the following best describes where you lived while in
        college. (Check any which apply)

        ____ Fraternity or equivalent.
        ____ Dormitory or other campus housing.   [____]
        ____ Off-campus room, apartment, house.   30
        ____ With my parents.
        ____ Other (Check and specify) _____

15.   Listed below are some purposes or results of college.
        Circle the one which was most important to you personally and,
        also, circle the one which you think was most important to the
        typical student. (Circle one in each column)

	Most important to me personally	Most important to the typical student
A basic general education and appreciation of ideas.	X	X
Having a good time while getting a degree.	X	X
Career training.	X	X
Developing the ability to get along with different kinds of people.	X	X

[____]
  31

16.   What is your feeling about the University of Minnesota. (Check one)
        ____ I have a very strong attachment to it.
        ____ I like it, but my feelings are not strong.   [____]
        ____ Mixed feelings.   32
        ____ I do not like it much, but my feelings are not strong.
        ____ I thoroughly dislike it.

****

YOUR PARENTS

****

17.   Parents' education. (Check appropriate level for each parent)

	MOTHER	FATHER
Less than 8th grade	____	____
8th grade	____	____
Some high school.................	____	____
High-school graduate.............	____	____
Technical or business, etc........	____	____
Some college.....................	____	____
College graduate.................	____	____
Some graduate or professional work.	____	____
Received advanced degree..........	____	____

[___]
33

[___]
34

****

WHILE YOU WERE IN COLLEGE

****

18.   Father's occupation _____   [___]
                                                                          35

        Mother's occupation _____

19.   How would you describe your parents' economic status in comparison
        with that of your classmate's parents. (Check one)

____   Very much poorer
____   Poorer
____   About average   [___]
____   Fairly well-off   36
____   Well-to-do

20.   When you were growing up, how would you describe your feelings
        toward your family and home situation. (Check one)

____   I was very happy with the way things were.
____   I was happier than average.   [___]
____   About average.   37
____   I was more unhappy than average.
____   I was very unhappy.

21.   Did your parents think it was important for you to get a college
        education. (Check one)

____   Thought it extremely important.
____   Thought it was all right.
____   They were neutral.   [___]
____   They were somewhat opposed to the idea.   38
____   They were very opposed to the idea.

****

CURRENT STATUS OF YOUR PARENTS

****

22.   Living   Deceased   YOUR AGE at time of death   [___]
                                                                          39
        Father _____   _____   _____ years
        Mother _____   _____   _____ years   [___]
                                                                          40

23.   Parents' marital status (current or at time of death)

                              YOUR AGE at the time

        _____ Married
        _____ Divorced   _____
        _____ Separated   _____   [___]
        _____ Mother remarried   _____   41
        _____ Father remarried   _____   [___]
                                                                     42

24.   How many brothers and sisters did you have.

        A.   OLDER brothers _____ OLDER sisters _____   [I   ]
                                                                  43   44
        B.   YOUNGER brothers ____ YOUNGER sisters _____

                                                                 [I   ]
25.   How many of your brothers and sisters are college   45   46
        graduates.   [___]
                _____   47

26.   Religion:

        A.   In which were you reared. (Check one)
                _____ Protestant (Check and specify) _____)   [___]
                _____ Roman Catholic   48
                _____ Jewish
                _____ Other (Check and specify)_____)
                _____ None

        B.   Your present preference. (Check one)
                _____ Protestant (Check and specify) _____)   [___]
                _____ Roman Catholic   49
                _____ Jewish
                _____ Other (Check and specify) _____)
                _____ None

Leave this
column blank

****

YOUR PRESENT WIFE   (If never married, skip to Question 29)

****

27.   WIFE'S EDUCATION:

Check highest educational level reached
and fill in appropriate blanks.

	DEGREE	SCHOOL NAME	LOCATION

_____ Less than 8th grade.   [___]
_____ 8th grade.   50
_____ Some high school.
_____ High-school graduate.
_____ Tech. or business, etc. _____ _____ _____ [___]
                                                                                  51
_____ Some college.   _____ _____ _____

_____ College graduate.   _____ _____ _____

_____ Some graduate or pro-   _____ _____ _____
      fessional training.

_____ Received advanced   _____ _____ _____
      degree.

28.   Wife's current occupation: _____

A.   She is _____ is not _____ employed outside the home.   [___]
                                                                          52

B.   If your wife is employed, would you briefly characterize   [___]
     her job and her job responsibilities: 53

     Job Title _____

     Responsibilities: _____

     _____

     _____

****

YOUR CHILDREN

****

E D U C A T I O N

NAME (First, Middle)	AGE	SEX	HIGH SCHOOL Name & Location	GRAD?	COLLEGE Name & Location	GRAD?	DEGREE	EMPLOYMENT	Any Outstanding Achievements: (Awards Elected Offices Scholarships Honor Society Etc.)

****

YOUR CURRENT OCCUPATION

****

NOTE: If you are unemployed or retired, please answer
this section as you would for your major occupation.

29.   Job Title: _____   [___]
                                                                        54

30.   Employer: _____   [___]
                                                                        55

31.   Please give a brief description of work performed, or how your
time is spent:

_____

_____

32.   Which of the following best describes your current employment
situation. (Check all that apply)

____ Unemployed.
____ Disabled.   [___]
____ Retired.   56
____ Company with 100 or more employees.
____ Company with fewer than 100 employees.
____ Professional partnership.   [___]
____ Family business.   57
____ Self-employed.
____ Research organization or institute.
____ College or University or Junior College.
____ Elementary or secondary school or school system.
____ Other educational institutions; (e.g., technical, vocational school)
____ Federal Government (U.S.)
____ State or Local government
____ Hospital, Church, Clinic, Welfare organization, etc.
____ Other (Check and specify: _____)

PLEASE CHECK AS APPLICABLE TO YOU:

33.   My work is in: ____ the same field I studied in college.   [___]
                         ____ a different but related field.   58
                         ____ an entirely different, unrelated field.

34.   I decided on my present type of work _____   [___]
attending undergraduate college.   before   while   after   59

35.   Length of time you have worked at your present position: _____   [___]
                                                        Years   60

36.   Length of time you have worked at this type of work: _____   [___]
                                                        Years   61

37.   Number of employees you supervise, or are directly responsible: _____   [___]
                                                                                    62

38.   Number of hours per week on the average you spend on your job: _____   [___]
                                                                                    63

39.   Relationship to supervisor:

       I have no supervisor: _____

                     _____ very closely with
       I work   _____ moderately closely with   my supervisor.   [___]
                     _____ fairly independently with   64
                     _____ completely independently of

40.   If you were just starting out again, (after leaving college), which
       of these characteristics would be very important to you in choosing
       a job or career:

       CHECK AS MANY AS APPLY - CIRCLE MOST IMPORTANT ONE: [___]
                                                                                  65
            _____ Making a lot of money.
            _____ Opportunities to be original and creative.
            _____ Opportunities to be helpful to others or useful to society.
            _____ Avoiding a high-pressure job which takes too much out of you.
            _____ Living and working in the world of ideas.
            _____ Freedom from supervision in my work.
            _____ Opportunities for moderate but steady progress, rather than
                     the chance of extreme success or failure.
            _____ A chance to exercise leadership.
            _____ The opportunity to work in a specific geographic area.
            _____ Job security.
            _____ Opportunity to work with people rather than things.
            _____ Other (specify: _____
            _____)

41.   Please rate the following in terms of their effect on your career plans
       or decisions. (Circle one in each row)

		VERY IMPORTANT	FAIRLY	UNIM-PORTANT	REC'D NONE	
A.	Vocational or similar psychological tests:	X	X	X	X	[___] 66
B.	Discussions with my academic advisor:	X	X	X	X	[___] 67
C.	Discussions with faculty members other than my advisor:	X	X	X	X	[___] 68
D.	Advice from parents:	X	X	X	X	[___] 69
E.	Interviews with a professional psychological or vocational counselor:	X	X	X	X	[___] 70
F.	High-school teacher:	X	X	X	X	[___] 71

42.   Please rate yourself on the following dimensions as you really think
        you are. (Circle one in each row)

	VERY	FAIRLY	NEITHER	FAIRLY	VERY		
A. Unfavorable toward modern art.	X	X	X	X	X	Favorable toward modern art.	[___] 72
B. Politically liberal.	X	X	X	X	X	Polit. conserv.	[___] 73
C. Conventional in opinions and values.	X	X	X	X	X	Unconventional in opinions & values.	[___] 74
D. Religious	X	X	X	X	X	Non-religious	[___] 75

****

YOUR SATISFACTION WITH YOUR OCCUPATION

****

                In this section, we are trying to find out
                how well people like their work. We are
                asking you to distinguish between your oc-
                cupation (for example, chemist) and your
                specific job (for example, with the WIDJIT
                Chemical Company.)

        The first group of questions refers to your Occupation. Please answer them
        considering your Occupation - without thinking of your current Job situation.

43.   Check the following statement which best tells how well you like your
        Occupation.

                _____ I hate it.
                _____ I dislike it.
                _____ I don't like it.
                _____ I am indifferent to it.
                _____ I like it.
                _____ I am enthusiastic about it.
                _____ I could not be more satisfied.

44.   Check one of the following to show how much of the time you feel satis-
        fied with your Occupation.

                _____ All of the time.
                _____ Most of the time.
                _____ A good deal of the time.
                _____ About half of the time.
                _____ Occasionally
                _____ Seldom
                _____ Never

45.   Check one of the following which best tells how you feel about changing your Occupation:

_____ I would quit this Occupation at once if I could get anything else to do.
_____ I would enter almost any other Occupation in which I could earn as much as I am earning now.
_____ I am not eager to change my Occupation, but I would do so if I could get into a better Occupation.
_____ I cannot think of any Occupation for which I would exchange mine.
_____ I would not exchange my Occupation for any other.

46.   Check one of the following to show how you think you compare with other people:

_____ No one likes his Occupation better than I.
_____ I like my Occupation much better than most people like theirs.
_____ I like my Occupation better than most people like theirs.
_____ I like my Occupation about as well as most people like theirs.
_____ I dislike my Occupation more than most people dislike theirs.
_____ I dislike my Occupation much more than most people dislike theirs.
_____ No one dislikes his Occupation more than I.

47.   If you had your life to live over, would you choose the same Occupation?

_____ I am sure I would not.
_____ I doubt if I would.
_____ I might not.
_____ I don't know.
_____ I think I would.
_____ I'm quite sure I would.
_____ I'm sure I would.

48.   Would you suggest that a young person with the same abilities and interests that you have enter your Occupation?

_____ Very strongly.
_____ Yes, in most cases.
_____ Probably.
_____ If he could not get anything better.
_____ Not in most cases.
_____ No.

49.   How satisfied are you with the amount of prestige attached to your Occupation?

_____ very dissatisfied.
_____ somewhat dissatisfied.
_____ not quite satisfied.
_____ indifferent to it.
_____ satisfied.
_____ very well satisfied.
_____ completely satisfied.

50.   If you were to change your <u>Occupation</u> in the next five years,
       what do you think the reason would be?

    _____ To enter a more interesting <u>Occupation</u>.
    _____ To get more pay in a new <u>Occupation</u>.
    _____ To enter an <u>Occupation</u> with more prestige.
    _____ To gain more independence in my work.

51.   Which gives you more satisfaction? (Check one)

    _____ Your <u>Occupation</u>.

    _____ Equal satisfaction from <u>Occupation</u> and spare-time activities.

    _____ The things you do in your spare time.

    [_____]
            1-3

    [___]
     10

    [___]
     11

    [___]
     12

****

YOUR SATISFACTION WITH YOUR JOB

****

The next group of questions refers to your
present <u>Job Situation</u>; (e.g., working for
the University of Minnesota). As you answer, consider your specific job and the
things about it that you like or dislike.

52.   Choose the one of the following statments which best tells how well
       you like your <u>Job Situation</u>. (Place a check-mark in front of that
       statement.)

    _____ I hate it.
    _____ I dislike it.
    _____ I don't like it.
    _____ I am indifferent to it.
    _____ I like it.
    _____ I am enthusiastic about it.
    _____ I couldn't be more satisfied.

53.   Check one of the following to show how much of the time you feel
       satisfied with your <u>Job Situation</u>.

    _____ All of the time.
    _____ Most of the time.
    _____ A good deal of the time.
    _____ About half of the time.
    _____ Occasionally
    _____ Seldom
    _____ Never

54.   Check one of the following which best tells how you feel about changing your Job.

_____ I would quit this Job at once if I could get anything else to do.
_____ I would take almost any Job in which I would earn as much as I am earning now.
_____ I would like to exchange my present Job for another in the same line of work.
_____ I am not eager to change my Job, but I would do so if I could get into a better Job.
_____ I cannot think of any Job for which I would exchange mine.
_____ I would not exchange my Job for any other.

55.   Check one of the following to show how you think you compare with other people.

_____ No one likes his Job better than I like mine.
_____ I like my Job much better than most people like theirs.
_____ I like my Job better than most people like theirs.
_____ I like my Job about as well as most people like theirs.
_____ I dislike my Job more than most people dislike theirs.
_____ I dislike my Job much more than most people dislike theirs.
_____ No one dislikes his Job more than I dislike mine.

56.   If you had your life to live over, would you choose the same Job? (Check one)

_____ I am sure I would not.
_____ I doubt if I would.
_____ I might not.
_____ I don't know.
_____ I think I would.
_____ I am quite sure I would.
_____ I am sure I would.

57.   Would you suggest that a young person with the same abilities and interests that you have enter a Job Situation similar to yours?

_____ Very strongly.
_____ Yes, in most cases.
_____ Probably.
_____ If he could not get anything better.
_____ Not in most cases.
_____ No.

58.   How satisfied are you with the amount of prestige attached to your Job? (Check one)

_____ very dissatisfied.
_____ somewhat dissatisfied.
_____ not quite satisfied.
_____ indifferent to it.
_____ satisfied.
_____ very well satisfied.
_____ completely satisfied.

Leave this
column blank

59.   Which gives you more satisfaction? (Check one)

_____ Your Job.
_____ Equal satisfaction from Job and spare-time activities.
_____ Things you do in your spare time.

[___I___]
  13 14

[___I___]
  15 16

[___]
 17

****

YOUR EMPLOYMENT HISTORY

****

In the next few pages, we are asking you
about your previous jobs. We are particularly concerned with:

Are people in occupations closely
related to their college training?

Why do people change jobs?

At about what point in life is the
final occupation chosen? Etc.

60.   Since leaving college, how many times have you been unemployed longer
than two weeks. _____ Times.

[___]
 18

61.   About how many months (totally) since you left college have you been
unemployed. (Do not include long vacations, etc., that you took by
choice.) _____ Months

[___]
 19

NOTE   The first page following asks about your FIRST JOB
AFTER LEAVING THE UNIVERSITY.

Please fill out one page for each job you have held
OVER SIX MONTHS, up to your current job.

If you have held more jobs than there are pages,
please use as many blank sheets as necessary to provide us with the information on subsequent jobs.
Follow the outline as given on this form.

```
**********************
                              This page is for the first full-time
YOUR EMPLOYMENT HISTORY       job you held after leaving the University.
                              If it is the same job that you hold cur-
**********************        rently, skip to Question 81.
```

62. Job Title (and/or Rank) _____

63. Duties: (How you spent your time) _____   [___]
                                                                            20
     _____

64. Number of employees you supervised or were directly responsible:_____   [___]
                                                                              21
65. Please check as applicable.

     The work was: _____ very closely related to my field of study in college.
                   _____ in a related but different field.   [___]
                   _____ not at all related to my field of study in college.   22

66. Dates of employment: FROM _____ TO _____ Total years _____   [___]
                                                                               23
67. Approximate salary or income: Starting $ _____   [___]
                                                                               24
                                      Leaving $ _____   [___]
                                                                               25
68. Did you receive any promotions while on this job? NO _____ YES _____

     If YES, specify. _____
                                                                              [___]
     _____   26

69. Reasons for leaving this job or business. (Check all those which apply -
                                      Circle the one most important)

     ____ Return to school   ____ Was offered better job elsewhere
     ____ Military service   ____ Not enough financial return
     ____ Service discharge   ____ No opportunity for advancement   [___]
     ____ Health   ____ Did not like the work   27
     ____ Business decline, laid off ____ Did not like the people
     ____ Fired   ____ Did not like the location   [___]
     ____ Job was too demanding   ____ Work was not challenging enough   28
                                      ____ Other (specify) _____

70. Please check as applicable, distinguishing between Occupation and the
     particular Job; for example, between being a chemist and working at the
     Widjit Chemical Company. (Place one check in each column)

     OCCUPATION   JOB   FEELING: [___]
     _____   _____   29
     _____   _____   I very much liked it.

     _____   _____   I was moderately satisfied.

     _____   _____   I was moderately dissatisfied.

     _____   _____   I very much disliked it.
```
```

****

YOUR EMPLOYMENT HISTORY   This page is for the next
                                 full-time job you held.
****

71. Job Title (and/or Rank) _____

72. Duties: (How you spent your time) _____
                                                                        [___]
     _____   30

73. Main reasons for selecting this job over the previous job:
     (Check ALL that apply and Circle the ONE most important)
                                                                        [___]
     _____ Higher pay   _____ Better geographical location   31
     _____ Less pressure   _____ More challenging work
     _____ More security   _____ More time for family
     _____ More freedom   _____ No choice - only job available
     _____ More prestige   _____ More chance for promotion
     _____ More interesting   _____ Other (specify) _____

     _____

74. Number of employees supervised or directly responsible for: _____   [___]
                                                                              32
75. The work was: _____ very closely related to my field of study in college.
                   _____ in a related but different field.
                   _____ not at all related to my field of study in college.

76. Employment dates: FROM _____ TO _____ Total Years _____   [___]
                                                                           33
77. Approximate salary or income: Starting $_____ Leaving $_____ [___I___]
                                                                          34   35
78. Did you receive any promotions while on this job? NO _____ YES _____

     If YES, specify: _____
                                                                        [___]
     _____   36

79. Reasons for leaving: (Check all those applying - Circle the one most
                          important)
     _____ Return to school   _____ Was offered better job elsewhere
     _____ Military service   _____ Not enough financial return   [___]
     _____ Service discharge   _____ No opportunity for advance   37
     _____ Health   _____ Did not like the work
     _____ Business decline/laid off _____ Did not like the people
     _____ Fired   _____ Did not like the location   [___]
     _____ Job was too demanding   _____ Work was not challenging enough   38
     _____ Other (specify)

     _____

80. Please check as applicable, distinguishing between Occupation and the
     particular Job; for example, between being a chemist and working at
     the Widjet Chemical Company. (Place one check in each column)

     OCCUPATION   JOB   FEELING:

      _____   _____   I very much liked it.

      _____   _____   I was moderately satisfied.
                                                                        [___]
      _____   _____   I was moderately dissatisfied.   39

      _____   _____   I very much disliked it.

Next
section
starts
here.
Q.81

****

AWARDS, HONORS, ETC.

****

81. Please indicate your achievements or honors you have won, [_____]
and total the number in each category: 1-3

		TOTAL NUMBER	[___]
			10
____	Fiction articles and books published.	____	[___]
			11
____	Technical articles or books published.	____	[___]
			12
____	Other non-fiction articles and books published.	____	[___]
			13
____	Patents	____	[___]
			14
____	Other publications: (Specify)	____	[___]
			15
	_____		
____	Awards for Art.	____	[___]
			16
____	Awards for Music.	____	[___]
			17
____	Awards for dramatic productions and performances.	____	[___]
			18
____	Armed Forces Service Medals and decorations awarded on individual basis (Silver Star, Purple Heart, etc.) (Do not include theater ribbons, unit awards, etc.)	____	[___]
			19
____	Civic awards.	____	[___]
			20
____	Professional or Business awards.	____	[___]
			21
____	Athletic awards.	____	[___]
			22
____	Invitational Addresses; (i.e., Wm. James lecture at Harvard).	____	[___]
			23
____	Other. (Please think carefully and specify any other awards and honors you have won.)	____	[___]
			24

_____

_____

_____

_____

_____

82.   Has your wife received any awards or recognition for anything of
      the above nature? If so, what?   [I   ]
                                                                          25   26

      _____

      _____

      _____

      _____

      _____

83.   Have you ever been on television?   [   ]
                                                                           27
            NO _____

            YES _____   If YES, how many times: _____

                            For what reasons: _____

                            _____

                            _____

                            _____

                            _____

84.   How many speeches have you given in the past two years?
      (Include papers read at professional meetings) _____   [   ]
                                                                           28

****

ORGANIZATIONS AND ACTIVITIES

****

85.   In which of the following organizations are you an active
       participant, and about how many hours per month do you
       spend in this activity?

       Check any applicable and fill in number of hours:

ORGANIZATIONS   HOURS PER MONTH

_____ Union: (Engineers, carpenter, electrician, etc.)   _____   [____]
                                                                        29
_____ Professional: (AMA, Local Bar Assoc., APA, etc.)   _____   [____]
                                                                        30
_____ Business: (NAM, NOMA, Chamber of Commerce, etc.)   _____   [____]
                                                                        31
_____ Religious and Fellowships: (Masons, Knights of Columbus, _____ [____]
                              Shriners, etc.)   32

_____ Civic Groups: (PTA, Homeowners Assoc., Urban League, _____   [____]
                         Better Business Bureau, etc.)   33

_____ Service Clubs: (Kiwanis, Rotary, Lions, Elks, etc.)   _____   [____]
                                                                        34
_____ Political: (GOP, DFL, ADA, ACLU, etc.)   _____   [____]
                                                                        35
_____ Agricultural: (Farm Bureau, Grange, etc.)   _____   [____]
                                                                        36
_____ Charitable: (YMCA, Hospital Assoc., United Fund, etc.) _____   [____]
                                                                        37
_____ Religious services: (Church Board, B'nai B'rith, etc.) _____   [____]
                                                                        38
_____ Social: (Country Club, Athletic Club, etc.)   _____   [____]
                                                                        39
_____ Special Interest and Hobby Clubs: (Dance, Bridge,
       Model Train, Sports Car, etc.)   _____   [____]
                                                                        40
_____ Other (Please specify). _____   _____   [____]
                                                                        41
       _____

       _____

86.   Within the past two years, have you held any elected offices in
       any of the above?
                        NO _____

                        YES _____   If YES, please specify: [___I___]
                                                                    42   43

       _____

       _____

****
YOUR ECONOMIC STATUS
****

In this section, we would like to ask you
about your current economic status. This
is a very personal area, but we would like
very much to have some idea of how college
freshmen of the 1930's are doing in today's
economy. Of course, none of this individual information will be released to anyone.

Please place checks in the appropriate places and fill in where necessary.

87. _____ Renter   If RENTER, rent paid: $_____/   [___]
                                                                             44

    _____ Home Owner If HOME OWNER, the current market value of my

                      home is approximately: $_____ $ _____   *[___]
                                                                             45

                      The range of values, or the average market value of
                      residences in my neighborhood is approximately:

                                            $ _____   [___]
                                                                             46

88. _____ I do
                      ] have a summer cabin or other type of second home.   [___]
    _____ I do not   47

89. Amount of life insurance carried on your life:

              INCLUDE ONLY "PERSONAL" INSURANCE, NOT THAT
              CARRIED ON YOU AS A PROTECTION FOR YOUR
              BUSINESS. INCLUDE GROUP-INSURANCE PLANS...

    _____ NONE   _____ $50,001 to $100,000
    _____ Less than $10,000   _____ $100,001 to $200,000   [___]
    _____ $10,001 to $20,000   _____ More than $200,001   48
    _____ $20,001 to $50,000

90. What is your total family yearly income before taxes:

              (Include both your own and your wife's salary,
              income from investments, rent, etc.)

    $ _____ Per year to the nearest thousand.   [___]
                                                                            49

91.   Approximately, what per-cent fall in each of the following categories?
       (Just enter amount if that is easier than calculating percentages)

_____ Own salary (include commissions, etc.)

_____ Your wife's salary.

_____ Royalties.

_____ Rent from property.   [___]
                                                                        50
_____ Dividends, trust funds, interest on savings, etc.

_____ Stock and bond sales.

_____ Consulting and speaking fees.

_____ Other (Specify) _____

        100% TOTAL

92.   About how much would you estimate your current estate to be?

              (Include value of home, other property owned,
              cash value of insurance policies, stocks and
              bonds, business owned, other valuables, etc.)

       $ _____   Roughly, what per-cent of this   [___]
                                  is due to inherited wealth?   51

                                          _____ %   [___]
                                                                        52

93.   We would like to have some idea of trends over the years. Could you
       indicate your approximate annual income before taxes for each of the
       years indicated below. (Do not include wife's income.)

                         ANNUAL INCOME

              1940 $ _____   [___]
                                                                      53
              1945 $ _____   [___]
                                                                      54
              1950 $ _____   [___]
                                                                      55
              1955 $ _____   [___]
                                                                      56
              1960 $ _____   [___]
                                                                      57

****

REST AND RELAXATION

****

In this section we are interested in the things you do in your spare time. (Yes, we know. We don't have much either.)

READING:

94.   What kind of reading do you most enjoy?

_____   [___]
                                                    58
_____

95.   About how many books would you say you have read in the past 12 months?

                                        _____   [___]
                                                    59

96.   Roughly, how many books totally, would you estimate you own?

                                        _____   [___]
                                                    60

97.   About how many books do you buy in a typical 12-month period?

                                        _____   [___]
                                                    61

98.   Which of these Magazines do you subscribe or buy regularly?

____ American Home	____ Parents' Magazine
____ Argosy	____ Popular Mechanics
____ Atlantic Monthly	____ Popular Science
____ Better Homes & Gardens	____ Reader's Digest
____ Capper's Farmer	____ Redbook
____ Coronet	____ Saturday Evening Post
____ Fortune	____ Science
____ Farm Journal	____ Scientific American
____ Good Housekeeping	____ Sports Afield
____ Harper's	____ Sports Illustrated
____ Holiday	____ Successful Farming
____ Ladies Home Journal	____ The Farmer
____ Life	____ Time
____ Look	____ True
____ McCall's	____ U. S. News & World Report
____ Nation	____ Other (Specify)
____ National Geographic	
____ National Review	
____ New Republic	
____ Newsweek	
____ New Yorker	

[___]   62

[___]   63

[___]   64

Which Newspapers do you subscribe or buy regularly?

LOCAL: _____   [___]
                                                   65

OTHER: _____

100.   Have you ever written a letter to the editor?

        ____ No   ____ Did it once or twice.   ____ Do it reasonably often.   [___]
                                                                                  66

101.   Have you ever written a letter to your Senator, Congressman, or any
        other government representative?

        ____ No   ____ Did it once or twice.   ____ Do it reasonably often.   [___]
                                                                                  67

102.   About how often do you watch television?

        ____ Never   ____ 2-5 hours daily.
        ____ Less than 1 hour weekly.   ____ 6-10 hours daily.   [___]
        ____ About 2-5 hours weekly.   ____ More than 10 hours daily.   68
        ____ About 1 hour daily.

103.   List the two or three television programs you watch most regularly
        and Circle your favorite one. (This is one area where individuals
        frequently list some "intellectual" programs that they think they
        should watch. If GUNSMOKE or HUCKLEBERRY HOUND are your favorites,
        do not be ashamed to say so.)   [___]
                                                                                  69
        _____

        _____

        _____

104.   Do you ever attend lectures of various sorts: scientific, art,
        foreign affairs, community forums, etc. other than those connected
        with your work?   [___]
                                                                                  70
        ____ No   ____ Yes   If YES, what kind of affairs do you attend:

        _____

105.   About how often do you go to movies?   [___]
                                                                                  71
        ____ Twice a week or more   ____ Once every few months
        ____ Once a week   ____ Once a year
        ____ Once every two weeks   ____ Never
        ____ Once a month

106.   About how often do you go to plays?   [___]
                                                                                  72
        ____ Twice a week or more   ____ Once every few months
        ____ Once a week   ____ Once a year
        ____ Once every two weeks   ____ Never
        ____ Once a month

107.   What kind of music do you most enjoy? _____   [___]
                                                                                  73
        _____

108.   Do you own a hi-fi?

    ____ No   ____ Yes, I have ____ Monaural   ____ Stereo   ____ FM Tuner   [___]
    74

109.   About how many phonograph records do you own, roughly? _____   [___]
    75

110.   About how many phonograph records do you purchase in a typical 12-
    month period?   _____   [___]
    76

111.   How many concerts do you attend in a typical 12-month period? ___   [___]
    77

112.   Does your home contain paintings, sketches, prints, statues, or
    anything of that sort?

    ____ No   ____ Yes   If YES, how many would you estimate? _____   [___]
    78

113.   Have you purchased anything of this nature in the past 12 months?

    ____ No   ____ Yes   If YES, about how many? _____   [___]
    79

114.   What about sports?

A. Please list those sporting activities that you attend as a spectator:

    _____   [___]
    80

    _____

    _____   [_____]
    1-3

B. List sports that you participate in reasonably often: [___]
    10

    _____

    _____

115.   About how often do you attend sporting events?

    ____ Twice a week or more   ____ Very irregularly
    ____ Once a week   [___]
    ____ Twice a month   ____ Never   11

116.   About how often do you participate in any sport?

    ____ Daily   ____ Twice a month
    ____ Twice a week   ____ Very irregularly   [___]
    ____ Once a week   ____ Never   12

117.   Please list other hobbies, interests, or leisure-time activities
        which you spend time; for example, gardening, collections, photo-
        graphy, that have not been covered above: [___]
                                                                            13
        _____

        _____

        _____

118.   About how much time a week do you spend on these? _____Hours   [___]
                                                                            14

****

    YOUR HEALTH

****

119.   Height: _____ Weight: _____   We will keep this confidential, [___]
                                             of course.   15
                                                                            [___]
                                                                            16
120.   Approximately, how many days of work have you missed because of ill-
        ness in the last two years?
                (For those not regularly working, answer as if you
                had a full-time job outside your home.)   _____   [___]
                                                                            17

121.   How many times have you gone to the doctor in the past two years?___
        For what reasons:

        ____ Check-Up   ____ General advice
        ____ Major surgery   ____ General health advice
        ____ Physical illness   ____ Other (Please specify)   [___]
        ____ Serious accident   18
        ____ Emotional disturbance
                                   _____

122.   Have you been hospitalized (for either physical or emotional reasons?

        ____ No   ____ Yes   How many times? _____   [___]
                                                                            19
                   If YES [For how long?   _____

                               For what reasons?_____

                               _____

                               _____

                               _____

123. Do you have any particular physical or health trouble?

_____ No _____ Yes

If YES, please check appropriate space: [___]
                                                                            20

_____ Asthma or Hay Fever   _____ Physical disability (Specify)
_____ Cancer
_____ Diabetes   _____
_____ Emotional disorder
_____ Heart condition   _____
_____ High-blood pressure
_____ Multiple Sclerosis   _____ Other (Please specify):
_____ Nervousness
_____ Ulcers   _____

                                    _____

124. Please check if you use any of the following prescription drugs:
_____ Sedatives   _____ Other (Please specify):
_____ Tranquilizers
_____ Sleeping pills   _____   [___]
_____ Energizers (Dexadrine, Benzadrine,   21
           etc.)

IF USED, about how often?

_____ Every day   _____ Once or twice a month
_____ Several times a week   _____ Less than once a month
_____ Once or twice a week   [___]
                                                                        22

125. What is your present state of health?

_____ Poor - (If so, is this a usual state? _____ or a temporary
_____ Fair   state? _____   [___]
_____ Average   23
_____ Excellent

126. Do you have a family doctor?   _____ No _____ Yes   [___]
                                                                        24

127. Have you ever gone to a psychiatrist or psychologist?
_____ No   _____ Yes - If YES, how long ago was that? _____   [___]
              If YES, length of time you saw him? _____   25

128. Since you entered college, has a health problem (either your own or
other persons' in the family) significantly affected your subsequent
life?   [___]
        _____ No   _____ Yes If YES, please specify details: 26

_____

_____

_____

T H E   E N D

Thank you for completing this Herculean
task. We intend to make the summary results of   data available to all the
participants who are interested in it.

Would you like to receive a summary report of this study?

      _____   NO

      _____   YES

[___]
27

Concerning the interest inventory and
scholastic aptitude test we are asking
you to complete, would you like to receive a personal report of your results?

      _____   NO

      _____   YES

[___]
28

_____

Date Completed

[___]
29

Return questionnaire to:
Dr. David Campbell
University of Minnesota
101 Eddy Hall
Minneapolis 14, Minnesota

APPENDIX II

UNIVERSITY OF MINNESOTA

.

RESEARCH INTERVIEW FORM

1962

David Campbell, Ph. D.
Theo. Volsky, Ph. D.

INSTRUCTIONS TO INTERVIEWER

1. PLEASE READ THROUGH THE INTERVIEW FORM BEFORE BEGINNING AN INTERVIEW.

2. The form will be used on men and women, married and single, employed, retired and never employed, with and without children. Consequently, you will be required to use your own judgment in phrasing some of the questions and in asking or omitting some of the questions.

3. The notes on the left side of the page are for your information only and are not to be read to the subject. They give you further directions, give examples of expected and/or acceptable responses, give the purpose of the question, etc.

4. The questions to be read to the subject are in CAPITAL LETTERS on the right side of the page. Only that which is in CAPITAL LETTERS on the right side of the page is to be read aloud.

5. Respondent's possible answers are in small letters with a short line preceding them. Place a check before the appropriate answer and/or write in comments the person may have. Avoid writing in the far right column. That space is for tabulating.

6. Do not read aloud that which is in parentheses and lower case on the right hand side of the page--this is further directions for you in asking subsequent questions.

7. Exercise judgment in probing. Most areas to be probed are indicated. You will have to phrase your own probes depending upon what respondent has said. Try not to influence answers by suggesting possible replies. Restate the question without adding anything new, or ask the person to be more specific, to give examples, to tell you a little more about it, etc., or just wait--looking expectantly at the person.

8. It is important that the person be interviewed alone, in a relatively quiet place, without interruptions. It is especially important that spouse or children not be present due to the nature of some of the questions.

9. At one point, you will administer a 50 minute test. Therefore, you are advised to bring along some reading material or something you can do quietly. Also, at this time, you should consider the rating scale which is inserted at that point and begin making your judgments. Do not make your final judgment until you have completed the interview.

10. Please read through the interview form before beginning an interview.

Interviewer: THIS SHEET IS FOR YOUR USE ONLY.

Subject's Name_____

(_____)
1-3

We would like to have your "clinical impression" of the person interviewed. Rate the individual on the scales below by circling one number on each scale. The scales run from Poor (1) through Fair (2), Average (3), Good (4), to Excellent (5).

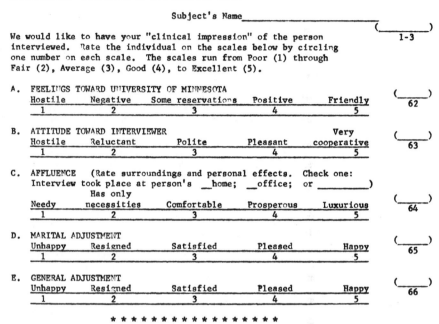

A. FEELINGS TOWARD UNIVERSITY OF MINNESOTA

Hostile	Negative	Some reservations	Positive	Friendly
1	2	3	4	5

(_____)
62

B. ATTITUDE TOWARD INTERVIEWER

Hostile	Reluctant	Polite	Pleasant	Very cooperative
1	2	3	4	5

(_____)
63

C. AFFLUENCE   (Rate surroundings and personal effects. Check one: Interview took place at person's __home; __office; or _____)

Needy	Has only necessities	Comfortable	Prosperous	Luxurious
1	2	3	4	5

(_____)
64

D. MARITAL ADJUSTMENT

Unhappy	Resigned	Satisfied	Pleased	Happy
1	2	3	4	5

(_____)
65

E. GENERAL ADJUSTMENT

Unhappy	Resigned	Satisfied	Pleased	Happy
1	2	3	4	5

(_____)
66

* * * * * * * * * * * * * * * * * *

The following scales are not "good" at one end and "bad" at the other (as above), but are bipolar, with the ends the extremes of much or little, or of opposites; the middle range being the average, the unremarkable, the "normally good," or "to be expected." Circle one number on each scale.

F. ACCESSIBILITY

Much unsolicited personal information given..		..........Open, frank..........			Defensive, denying	
1	2	3	4	5	6	7

(_____)
67

G. RATE & LEVEL OF ACTIVITY -- MANNER

Phlegmatic......	.Composed................		..Quick..		.Dynamic...Manic	
1	2	3	4	5	6	7

(_____)
68

H. SELF-CONFIDENCE

Inadequacy feelings.......	......Positive self-concept.....				.....Overbearing	
1	2	3	4	5	6	7

(_____)
69

I. ANXIETY LEVEL

Tense, worried..	.........Poised, at ease........			.	Unconcerned, Listless	
1	2	3	4	5	6	7

(_____)
70

Comments on the interview as a whole   _____

(_____)
71

Interviewer's Name

Introduction

Identify yourself as a representative of the University of Minnesota.
Refer to letters from the University to the person. Canfirm that person
is the subject sought, ie., entered the University of Minnesota in 1933-
1936 as a freshman.

Purpose of the Project   (Read to the subject):

JUST TO REFRESH YOUR MEMORY AS TO THE PURPOSE OF THIS PROJECT, IT

IS A LONG-TERM FOLLOW-UP ON PEOPLE WHO ENTERED COLLEGE DURING THE

DEPRESSION. BASICALLY, WE ARE ATTEMPTING TO INCREASE OUR ABILITY TO HLEP

YOUNG PEOPLE WITH REGARD TO COLLEGE ATTENDANCE, COLLEGE PROGRAM, AND

SUBSEOUENT POST-COLLEGE SUCCESS AND SATISFACTION.

Uniqueness of the Project   (Read to subject):

SUCH A FOLLOW-UP, WHICH GOES BACK 25-30 YEARS, WILL BE ONE OF THE

FIRST OF ITS KIND. THE UNIQUENESS AND IMPORTANCE OF THE PROJECT REOUIRES

ANSWERS WHICH ARE, MORE THAN THE AVERAGE, FRANK, STRAIGHTFORWARD, AND

COMPLETE. SOME OF THE QUESTIONS MAY SEEM SILLY OR OBVIOUS TO YOU: SOME

MAY SEEM PETTY OR PERSONAL. YOUR ANSWERS WILL SUPPLY INFORMATION, HOWEVER

WHICH WILL BE VERY IMPORTANT IN INCREASING OUR ABILITY TO EDUCATE OUR

YOUNG PEOPLE MORE EFFECTIVELY.

Confidential   (Read to the subject):

OF COURSE, ALL OF YOUR ANSWERS WILL BE HELD STRICTLY CONFIDENTIAL.

IF I JUST START, YOU'LL SEE WHAT WE'RE TRYING TO FIND OUT AND HOW

IT GOES!

NAME OF SUBJECT _____   (_____)
                First   Middle   Maiden   Last   1-3

NAME OF INTERVIEWER _____
                    First   Middle   Last

TIME INTERVIEW BEGAN_____

The purpose of questions 1-4 is to enable you to
phrase later questions appropriately--questions
dealing with work, marriage, family, etc. So
keep these answers in mind.

  1-a. ARE YOU MARRIED?

     ___yes (If yes, ask Q. 1-c)   (_____)
    b. ___no (If no) HAVE YOU EVER BEEN MARRIED?   11

      ___no
     c. ___yes (If yes) DO YOU HAVE ANY
      CHILDREN?   (_____)
          12

       ___no
      d. ___yes (If yes) BOYS OR GIRLS,
       AND WHAT ARE THEIR AGES?

       sex: ___ ___ ___ ___ ___

       age: ___ ___ ___ ___ ___

Record all answers verbatim if possible.

Paraphrase as little as possible

Select key phrases from the response for recording
long answers.

  2-a. ARE YOU NOW EMPLOYED?

    b. ___yes (If yes) WHAT IS YOUR OCCUPATION?   (_____)
          13

    _____

    c. ___no (If no) HAVE YOU EVER BEEN EMPLOYED
      OUTSIDE THE HOME SINCE LEAVING COLLEGE?

      ___no
    d. ___yes (If yes) WHAT WAS YOUR MAJOR
      OCCUPATION?

    _____

3-a. DID YOU GRADUATE FROM COLLEGE?

     ___yes

b. ___no (If no) HOW LONG DID YOU GO TO COLLEGE?
     ___years

(____)
14

Try to get information without influencing what
person says. <u>Do not put words in his mouth!</u>

4. WHAT WAS YOUR MAJOR IN COLLEGE?_____

(____)
15

5. WHY DID YOU GO TO COLLEGE?_____

(____)
16

Intent: Liberal education? Career preparation?
Parents' choice? Socialization? Find a husband?

6-a. DO YOU THINK YOUR UNIVERSITY EXPERIENCE WAS
REALLY WORTH THE TIME, MONEY, AND EFFORT THAT
YOU SPENT?

Try to get more information than a superficial yes/no
answer.

Before probing, let person say what he wants. <u>Do not put
words in his mouth!</u>

b. ___no. WHY NOT?_____

(____)
17

c. ___yes. IN WHAT WAYS?_____

<u>eg</u>: helped me in my job; improved me personally;
should have worked instead; etc.

7-a. DID THE DEPRESSION HAVE ANY EFFECT ON YOUR EDUCA-
TION?

     ___.no.

b. ___yes. IN WHAT WAY?_____

(____)
18

<u>eg</u>: could not go to desired college: could not find
job so went to college.

8. (If not mentioned earlier) DID IT PREVENT YOU
FROM REACHING YOUR EDUCATIONAL GOAL?

(_____)

___no.   ___yes.   19

9. WHAT EFFECT DID THE DEPRESSION HAVE ON YOU AFTER
YOU LEFT THE UNIVERSITY?

_____ (_____)

_____ 20

eg: Continued graduate work because of lack of job; was
unemployed for awhile; could not get job in desired area.

The next 6 questions are quite important to our study. Try
to do a particularly good job of probing and recording here.

10-a. IF YOU HAD IT TO DO OVER, WOULD YOU ENROLL IN THE
UNIVERSITY OF MINNESOTA AGAIN?

b. ___no.   WHAT WOULD YOU DO?_____ (_____)

_____ 21

c. ___yes.   WHY?_____

_____

11. WHAT COULD THE UNIVERSITY HAVE DONE DIFFERENTLY
THAT WOULD HAVE HELPED YOU MORE?

_____ (_____)

_____ 22

eg: more personal contact with faculty; emphasize
intellectual development; nothing; couldn't do what
I needed.

12. WHAT ASPECTS OF THE UNIVERSITY OF MINNESOTA--
ACTIVITIES, FACILITIES, ETC.--DO YOU FEEL
WERE PARTICULARLY WORTHWHILE, AND WHY?

(___I___)

_____ 23   24

_____

13. WHAT ARE YOUR MAIN CRITICISMS OF THE UNIVERSITY
PROGRAMS AS YOU EXPERIENCED THEM 25 YEARS AGO?

_____ (_____)

_____ 25

_____

_____

14. WHAT ARE YOUR MAIN CRITICISMS OF THE UNIVERSITY
     CURRENTLY?_____   (_____)
     _____   26

15-a. AS AN ADULT, HAS ANY UNIVERSITY OR COLLEGE HELPED
      OR BENEFITTED YOU IN ANY SPECIFIC WAY, SAY, IN
      THE LAST 5 YEARS?

        ___no.
     b. ___yes. WHICH SCHOOL?_____   (_____)
                                                         27
          c. WHAT HELP?_____
                                                      (_____)
          _____   28

eg: extension courses, services offered by various departments.

16. WHEN YOU WERE IN COLLEGE, DID YOU EVER DO ANY-
     THING FOR WHICH, IF YOU'D BEEN CAUGHT, YOU WOULD
     HAVE BEEN EXPELLED? YOU DON'T HAVE TO GIVE
     DETAILS--JUST THINK BACK AND ANSWER YES OR NO.

        ___yes.   ___no.   (_____)
                                                         29

17-a. DO YOU FEEL EVERYONE WHO HAS THE ABILITY SHOULD
      GO TO COLLEGE?

     b. ___no. WHY NOT?_____

        _____
                                                      (_____)
     c. ___yes. WHY DO YOU THINK SO?_____   30

        _____

18. WHICH DIRECTION, IF EITHER, SHOULD WE GO IN
     PROVIDING HIGHER EDUCATION FOR AMERICA'S TALENTED
     YOUTH: MAKE IT FREE TO ALL (AS WE DO SECONDARY
     SCHOOL) OR BY PERSONAL LOANS FROM THE GOVERNMENT
     TO CAPABLE INDIVIDUALS?

        ___neither   (_____)
        ___free to all   31
        ___government loans

        comments:_____

        _____
        _____
        _____

Ask 19-30 of all who are now employed, or have worked
at any job since leaving college. If never worked,
skip to Question 31.

> NOW I'D LIKE TO ASK YOU SOME QUESTIONS ABOUT YOUR
> WORK. (IF YOU HAVE WORKED AT ALL SINCE LEAVING
> COLLEGE, BUT ARE NOT NOW EMPLOYED, OR ARE RETIRED,
> PLEASE ANSWER AS YOU WOULD FOR YOUR MAJOR OCCUPATION.)

19. HOW DID YOU HAPPEN TO ENTER YOUR PRESENT
     OCCUPATION? (Pause. If necessary, say, HAD YOU
     ALWAYS PLANNED THIS, WAS IT HAPPENSTANCE, OR WAS
     IT A COMBINATION OF SEVERAL THINGS? Probe briefly.)

     _____ (_____)
                                                   32

20. IS YOUR WORK WHAT YOU THOUGHT IT WOULD BE BEFORE
     YOU BEGAN IN THIS FIELD?

     ___no.   ___yes.   (_____)
                                                   33
     comment:_____

     _____

21-a. GENERALLY SPEAKING, ARE YOUR INTERESTS TYPICAL
      OF OTHERS IN YOUR FIELD? (If necessary, say, DO
      YOU LIKE THE SAME KINDS OF PEOPLE, ACTIVITIES, ETC.)
      ___yes.

   b. ___no. HOW DO THEY DIFFER?_____ (_____)
                                                   34

     _____

Intent: generally interests of men in any occupation
can be differentiated from men in general. Does this
person feel he could be spotted this way?

22-a. IS YOUR WORK CLOSELY CONNECTED WITH WHAT YOU
      STUDIED IN COLLEGE?
                                                 (_____)
      ___yes   35

   b. ___no. WOULD YOU RATHER BE WORKING IN THE
              AREA YOU STUDIED?

          ___no.
      c. ___yes. WHAT PREVENTS YOU FROM DOING SO? (_____)
                                                      36

     _____

     _____

23.   WHAT INFLUENCED YOU IN CHOOSING YOUR PRESENT
      OCCUPATION?_____   (_____)
                                                              37
      _____

This is another important area. Probe diligently on
the next few questions.

24-a. DO YOU REMEMBER ANY ONE PERSON WHO WAS PARTICU_
      LARLY INFLUENTIAL IN ADVISING YOU ABOUT WHICH
      OCCUPATION YOU SHOULD ENTER?

      ___no.
   b. ___yes. WHO (WHAT RELATIONSHIP DID THEY HAVE   (_____)
      WITH YOU)?   38

      _____

25-a. DID YOU EVER RECEIVE ANY FORMAL VOCATIONAL
      COUNSELING WHILE YOU WERE IN COLLEGE?
                                                      (_____)
      ___no.   39
   b. ___yes. DO YOU REMEMBER WHAT THE COUNSELOR
      SAID?

         ___no.
      c. ___yes. WHAT?_____   (_____)
                                                     40
         _____

      d. DID IT HAVE ANY INFLUENCE ON YOUR LIFE?
                                                  (_____)
         ___no.   41
      e. ___yes. IN WHAT WAY?_____

         _____

         _____

      f. DO YOU THINK THE COUNSELING WAS HELPFUL?

         ___no.   ___yes.   (_____)
                                                     42
         comments:_____

         _____

         _____

26-a. (If not mentioned previously) HAVE YOU EVER
HAD ANY CONTACT WITH THE UNIVERSITY TESTING
BUREAU OR STUDENT COUNSELING BUREAU AT THE
UNIVERSITY OF MINNESOTA?

___no.

b. ___yes. IN WHAT RESPECT?_____

(___)
43

_____

c. WAS IT HELPFUL?

(___)
44

___no.   ___ yes.

comments:_____

_____

27. WHAT ARE THE 2 or 3 MOST IMPORTANT ABILITIES
NECESSARY TO DO A REALLY GOOD JOB AT THE KIND
OF WORK YOU DO?

(1)_____

(___)
45

(2)_____

(___)
46

(3)_____

(___)
47

28. HOW WOULD YOU RANK YOURSELF ON EACH OF THESE
ABILITIES?

(1) (2) (3)

___ ___ ___   VERY GOOD
___ ___ ___   BETTER THAN AVERAGE
___ ___ ___   AVERAGE
___ ___ ___   NOT VERY GOOD

(___)
48

(___)
49

(___)
50

29-a. REGARDLESS OF HOW MUCH YOU LIKE YOUR WORK, IS
THERE SOME OTHER KIND OF WORK YOU'D RATHER BE
DOING?

___no.

b. ___yes. WHAT IS IT?_____

(___)
51

_____

c. WHY DO YOU THINK YOU WOULD LIKE THAT BETTER
THAN THE WORK YOU'RE DOING NOW?

(___)
52

_____

_____

_____

Ask married men only.

Then skip to page 14 to give the Minnesota Scholastic
Aptitude Test.

30-a. HOW DOES YOUR WIFE FEEL ABOUT YOUR WORK?_____   (___)
                                                                 53
_____

_____

b. (If not indicated above) DOES SHE THINK IT
   SUITS YOUR SKILLS AND INTERESTS?   (___)
                                                                 54
___yes.
c. ___no. WHAT KIND OF WORK OR WHAT POSITION
           DOES SHE THINK WOULD SUIT YOU BETTER?

_____

_____

Ask working mothers only, including those who are not now
employed but have worked since leaving college.

31. WHAT EFFECT DO YOU THINK YOUR WORKING HAS
     HAD ON THE DEVELOPMENT OF YOUR CHILDREN?

_____   (___)
                                                    55
_____

_____

Ask working women who are now or have been married Questions
32-35.

32. WHAT EFFECT DO YOU THINK WORKING HAS HAD ON
     YOUR MARRIAGE?_____   (___)
                                                       56
_____

Ask working women who are now or have been married.

33. HOW DOES (OR DID) YOUR HUSBAND FEEL ABOUT YOUR
     WORKING?_____   (___)
                                                         57
_____

_____

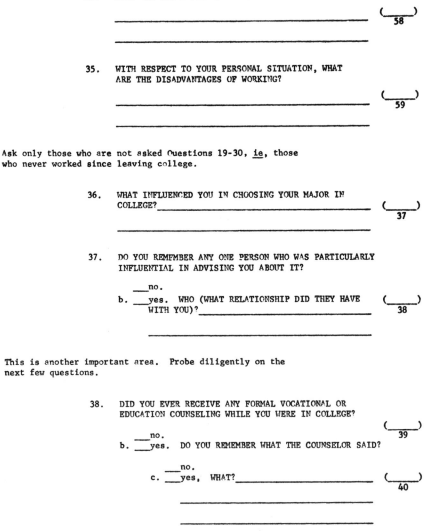

34.   WHAT ARE THE MAJOR ADVANTAGES OF WORKING?

_____   (_____)
                                                58
_____

35.   WITH RESPECT TO YOUR PERSONAL SITUATION, WHAT
      ARE THE DISADVANTAGES OF WORKING?

_____   (_____)
                                                59
_____

Ask only those who are not asked Questions 19-30, ie, those
who never worked since leaving college.

36.   WHAT INFLUENCED YOU IN CHOOSING YOUR MAJOR IN
      COLLEGE?_____   (_____)
                                                    37
_____

37.   DO YOU REMEMBER ANY ONE PERSON WHO WAS PARTICULARLY
      INFLUENTIAL IN ADVISING YOU ABOUT IT?

          ___no.
      b. ___yes. WHO (WHAT RELATIONSHIP DID THEY HAVE   (_____)
                   WITH YOU)?_____   38

      _____

This is another important area. Probe diligently on the
next few questions.

38.   DID YOU EVER RECEIVE ANY FORMAL VOCATIONAL OR
      EDUCATION COUNSELING WHILE YOU WERE IN COLLEGE?
                                                 (_____)
          ___no.   39
      b. ___yes. DO YOU REMEMBER WHAT THE COUNSELOR SAID?

              ___no.
      c. ___yes, WHAT?_____   (_____)
                                                   40
          _____

          _____

d. DID IT HAVE ANY INFLUENCE ON YOUR LIFE?

    ___no.

e. ___yes.   IN WHAT WAY?_____   (____)
                                       41

_____ _____

_____

f. DO YOU THINK THE COUNSELING WAS
   HELPFUL?
                                     (____)

    ___no.   ___yes.   42

    comments:_____

_____

_____

39-a. (If not mentioned previously,) HAVE YOU EVER HAD
     ANY CONTACT WITH THE UNIVERSITY TESTING BUREAU OR
     STUDENT COUNSELING BUREAU AT THE UNIVERSITY OF
     MINNESOTA?

    ___no.

b. ___yes.   IN WHAT RESPECT?_____   (____)
                                        43

_____

c. WAS IT HELPFUL?
                                   (____)

    ___no.   ___yes.   44

    comments:_____

_____

Ask women who are now or have been married Questions 40-41.

40.   WHAT ARE THE 2 OR 3 MOST IMPORTANT ABILITIES
     NECESSARY TO BE A GOOD WIFE & MOTHER?

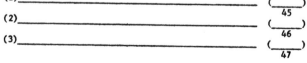

  (1)_____   (____)
                                       45
  (2)_____   (____)
                                       46
  (3)_____   (____)
                                       47

41. HOW WOULD YOU RANK YOURSELF ON EACH OF THESE
     ABILITIES?

    (1) (2) (3)

___	___	___	VERY GOOD	(____)
___	___	___	BETTER THAN AVERAGE	48
___	___	___	AVERAGE	(____)
___	___	___	NOT VERY GOOD	49

    (____)
     50

Ask unemployeed women who are now or have been married Questions
42-43.

42-a. DO YOU EVER WISH THAT YOU HAD (WORKED)
       (CONTINUED WORKING) AFTER LEAVING COLLEGE?

    ___no.

b. ___yes.   WHAT HAS STOOD IN YOUR WAY?_____

    (____)
     60

_____

_____

43-a. WOULD YOU LIKE TO (OR ARE YOU PLANNING TO) GET A
       JOB IN THE FUTURE?

    ___would not like to

b. ___would like to.   WHAT KIND OF WORK WOULD YOU
       LIKE TO DO?_____

    (____)
     61

_____

c. ___plan to.   WHAT KIND OF WORK DO YOU THINK YOU
       WILL DO?_____

_____

d. WHAT WOULD BE YOUR MAIN REASON FOR WORKING?___

    (____)
     62

_____

Ask all women.

44. DO YOU THINK A CAREER CAN BE AS SATISFYING AS
     MARRIAGE?

    ___no   ___yes

    (____)
     63

comments:_____

_____

_____

Give Minnesota Scholastic Aptitude Test at this point.

BEFORE WE GO ON, AT THIS POINT I WOULD LIKE TO HAVE YOU COMPLETE THE MINNESOTA SCHOLASTIC APTITUDE TEST. THIS IS THE CURRENT ENTRANCE TEST USED BY THE UNIVERSITY.

DR. CAMPBELL HAS TOLD US THAT ALMOST EVERYONE HAS SOME MISGIVINGS ABOUT THE TEST. BUT ON THE FEW CASES AVAILABLE, INDIVIDUALS HAVE ALMOST ALWAYS DONE BETTER THAN THEY DID 25 YEARS AGO, AND USUALLY DO VERY WELL IN COMPARISON WITH CURRENT FRESHMEN STUDENTS.

1. Give them opportunity to read directions (3-5 minutes or so).

2. Where directions say "...by blacking in the correct space..." (under #1, Reading) request that the person use a pencil (rather than a pen).

3. Make it very clear that they have 50 minutes, not an hour.

4. Give test.

5. Use a stopwatch or a watch with a second hand. Time exactly 50 minutes.

While the person is taking the test, remain as incomspicuous as possible.

You should use this time to look over the rating sheet we want you to fill out so that you can make the necessary observations.

You will have to make necessary adjustments in wording
for the specific situation.   (_____)
                                                                      1-3

Ask parents only.

              NOW I'D LIKE TO ASK YOU A LITTLE ABOUT YOUR
              CHILD (REN)'S EDUCATIONAL AND CAREER PLANS.

          45-a. WHAT ARE THE CURRENT PLANS FOR YOUR CHILD(REN)'S
                EDUCATION BEYOND HIGH SCHOOL?

                   ___none
              b. ___college. WHICH ONE OR WHAT TYPE? _____   (_____)
                                                                       11

                  _____

              c. ___other. (Probe.)_____

                  _____

Ask males.
          46. (IF YOU HAD A SON) WHAT CAREER OR TYPE OF CAREER
               DO YOU THINK WOULD BE BEST FOR (HIM) YOUR SON?

Ask females.
               (IF YOU HAD A DAUGHTER) WHAT CAREER OR TYPE OF
               CAREER DO YOU THINK WOULD BE BEST FOR (HER) YOUR
               DAUGHTER?

                  _____   (_____)
                                                                        12
                  _____

Ask parents.

          47. HAVE YOU EVER HAD ANY SERIOUS DISCUSSIONS WITH YOUR
               CHILD(REN) ABOUT (HIS)(HER)(THEIR) FUTURE CAREER(S)?

               ___no.   ___yes.   (_____)
                                                                       13
               comments:_____

                  _____

Ask males. 48. (IF YOU HAD A SON) WOULD YOU LIKE (HIM) YOUR SON
                 TO FOLLOW YOU IN YOUR OCCUPATION?

Ask females   (IF YOU HAD A DAUGHTER) WOULD YOU LIKE (HER) YOUR
                 DAUGHTER TO FOLLOW YOU IN YOUR OCCUPATION?

                 ___no.   ___yes.   (_____)
                                                                       14

49.   WHY DO YOU FEEL THIS WAY?_____   (_____)
                                                       15

_____

Questions 50-54 are for parents only.

Another important question.

50.   SUPPOSE (ONE OF)YOUR CHILD(REN) CHOSE A CAREER
      WHICH YOU FELT WAS COMPLETELY WRONG FOR (HIM)
      (HER) (THEM)--WHAT WOULD YOU DO?

      _____ (__I__)
                                                16 17
      _____

eg: Nothing; Try to talk him out of it; Forbid him to enter
it; Ask him to see counselor.

51-a. ARE ANY OF YOUR CHILDREN (IS YOUR CHILD) HAVING
      ANY REAL DIFFICULTY WITH SCHOOL WORK?

         ___no.
      b. ___yes. IN WHAT WAY?_____   (_____)
                                                     18

      _____

      c. WHAT DO YOU THINK IS THE REASON FOR THIS?_____
                                                        (_____)
      _____   19

52-a. HOW ABOUT SOCIALLY, ARE THEY (IS HE, IS SHE) HAVING
      ANY REAL DIFFICULTY WITH REGARD TO FRIENDS OR
      ANYTHING IN THE SOCIAL AREA?

         ___no.
      b. ___yes. IN WHAT WAY?_____   (_____)
                                                     20

      _____

      c. WHAT DO YOU THINK IS THE REASON FOR THIS?_____
                                                        (_____)
      _____   21

      _____

53-a. HAVE YOU HAD ANY (OTHER) SERIOUS PROBLEMS WITH
YOUR CHILDREN?

     ___no.
b. ___yes. TELL ME ABOUT THEM BRIEFLY_____   (___)
                                                22

_____

_____

54. MANY PEOPLE WOULD LIKE THEIR CHILDREN TO BE
DIFFERENT FROM THEMSELVES.

Ask males.   (IF YOU HAD A SON) HOW WOULD YOU LIKE (HIM) YOUR
SON TO BE DIFFERENT FROM YOU?

Ask females.   (IF YOU HAD A DAUGHTER) HOW WOULD YOU LIKE (HER)
YOUR DAUGHTER TO BE DIFFERENT FROM YOU?

_____   (I   )
                                                    23 24

_____

Responses will be coded in terms of self-satisfaction or
self-criticism, internalization (introspection) or
externalization (situational).

Ask all subjects.
                   WE'RE GOING TO ASK YOU A LITTLE ABOUT YOUR SOCIAL
LIFE.

55. DO YOU HAVE AS MANY SOCIAL CONTACTS AS YOU WOULD
LIKE, OR WOULD YOU RATHER HAVE MORE OR LESS?

___more. ___as many as I like. ___less.   (___)
                                                    25

56. IF YOU COULD, IN WHAT WAYS WOULD YOU CHANGE YOUR
SOCIAL LIFE?

_____(I   )
                                                   26 27

_____

_____

NOW LET'S CONTINUE ON A DIFFERENT TOPIC.

57 a. HAVE YOU EVER ACTIVELY CAMPAIGNED FOR A
      CANDIDATE FOR PUBLIC OFFICE?

       ___no
   b. ___yes. VERY OFTEN?   (___)
                                                            28

          ___once or twice
          ___often

58-a. HAVE YOU EVER RUN FOR A POLITICAL OFFICE?

       ___no.
   b. ___yes. FOR WHAT OFFICE?_____

        _____   (___)
                                                            29

       c. (If it is not apparent) WAS THIS
         LOCAL, STATE, OR NATIONAL?

         ___local. ___state. ___nat'l.   (___)
                                                            30

       d. WERE YOU ELECTED?

         ___no.   ___yes.   (___)
                                                            31

59-a. DID YOU EVER SERVE IN ANY CAPACITY AS A POLITICAL
      APPOINTEE, ADVISOR, OR ANYTHING OF THAT NATURE?

       ___no.
   b. ___yes. WHAT WAS YOUR TITLE?_____   (___)
                                                            32

        _____

       c. BRIEFLY, WHAT WERE YOUR DUTIES?

        _____   (___)
                                                            33

        _____

Try to get a specific statement.

    60.   GENERALLY SPEAKING, WHICH POLITICAL PARTY DO YOU
            USUALLY AGREE MOST WITH?
                              _____   (___)
                                                            34

Ask all who are now or have been married
questions 61-63.

> IN THE NEXT SECTION, I'D LIKE TO ASK YOU A FEW
> QUESTIONS ABOUT YOUR MARRIAGE.

Tact is essential in this area.   Probe
without prying.

61.   THINKING ABOUT YOUR OWN MARRIAGE, WHAT WOULD YOU
SAY ARE THE MAJOR REWARDS OF MARRIAGE?

_____   (_____)
                                                35

_____

62.   EVERY MARRIAGE HAS ITS GOOD AND BAD POINTS. WHAT
MAJOR DIFFICULTY WOULD YOU POINT TO AS THE ONE
HARDEST TO OVERCOME?

_____   (_____)
                                                36

_____

Probe sufficiently to rate the response.

63.   TAKING ALL THINGS TOGETHER, HOW WOULD YOU
DESCRIBE YOUR MARRIAGE: AS VERY SATISFYING,
ABOUT AVERAGE, OR NOT AS SATISFYING AS IT SHOULD
HAVE BEEN?

___very satisfying
___fairly satisfying   (_____)
___average   37
___fairly dissatisfying
___very dissatisfying

Ask all subjects.

> ONE OF THE AREAS WE'RE INTERESTED IN IS WHAT PEOPLE ARE
> CONCERNED ABOUT THESE DAYS.

64.   WHAT KINDS OF THINGS DO YOU WORRY ABOUT MOST?
(Probe)

_____   (_____)
                                                38

_____

eg: Yourself; Your family; your job;
the state of the world; etc.

65.   WE ALL TEND TO LABEL OUR OWN PERSONALITIES.
      WOULD YOU CLASSIFY YOURSELF AS A WORRIER?

Probe for degree on questions 65 & 66.

(___)
39

___a lot.   ___somewhat.   ___not very much.

66.   WOULD YOU SAY THAT YOU WORK UNDER A GREAT DEAL
      OF TENSION?

___yes.   ___somewhat.   ___no.

(___)
40

67-a. IN TIMES OF STRESS, WHAT PART DO YOU THINK YOUR
       EDUCATION PLAYS? (Probe.)

___no part

b. ___hinders)
                 IN WHAT WAYS?
c. ___helps)

(___)
41

_____

_____

eg: Person has become more sensitive;
Person has become more aware (Probe);
Person is better equipped to deal with
stress.

PROBLEMS OFTEN COME UP IN LIFE--PERSONAL PROBLEMS
CONCERNING FAMILY OR JOB OR MARRIAGE.

68-a. HAVE YOU EVER GONE TO A PROFESSIONAL PERSON FOR
       ADVICE AND HELP WITH ANY PERSONAL PROBLEM?

b. ___no.   DO YOU THINK YOU WOULD EVER HAVE A
            PERSONAL PROBLEM THAT GOT SO BAD YOU
            MIGHT WANT TO GO SOMEPLACE FOR HELP,
            OR DO YOU THINK YOU WOULD ALWAYS
            HANDLE THINGS LIKE THAT BY YOURSELF?

(___)
42

___seek help.   ___handle by self

comments:_____

_____

c. ___yes.   WOULD YOU TELL ME A LITTLE ABOUT THE
             REASON FOR SEEKING SUCH HELP?

(___)
43

_____

_____

          d. WHAT WAS THE SOURCE OF THIS HELP?

eg: Psychiatrist; Psychologist; Social   _____ (____)
worker; Minister; Teacher; etc. If an   44
agency is mentioned, probe for specific   _____
name. However, do not probe for
personal name.   _____

          e. HOW DID IT TURN OUT--DO YOU THINK
             IT HELPED IN ANY WAY?

Probe for explanation of simple yes/no.

                                               (____)
                                               45
           _____

           _____

          NOW I'D LIKE TO HAVE YOU THINK ABOUT YOUR WHOLE ADULT
          LIFE--HOW THINGS ARE NOW, HOW THEY WERE A FEW YEARS AGO,
          HOW THEY WERE WHEN YOU WERE IN COLLEGE.

    69.   WHEN YOU LEFT THE UNIVERSITY LIFE, WOULD YOU SAY
           YOU WERE AS SATISFIED WITH THE WAY THINGS WERE
           GOING FOR YOU AS THE AVERAGE COLLEGE STUDENT, OR
           WERE YOU MORE SATISFIED OR LESS SATISFIED?

           ___more.   ___same as the average.   ___less.   (____)
                                                         46

    70.   AND NOW--WOULD YOU SAY YOU ARE MORE SATISFIED,
           ABOUT AS SATISFIED, OR LESS SATISFIED AS COMPARED
           WITH MOST OF THE PEOPLE YOU ASSOCIATE WITH?

           ___more.   ___same as associates.   ___less.   (____)
                                                         47

    71.   COMPARED TO YOUR LIFE TODAY, HOW DO YOU THINK
           THINGS WILL BE 5 OR 10 YEARS FROM NOW--DO YOU
           THINK THINGS WILL BE MORE SATISFACTORY FOR YOU,
           NOT AS SATISFACTORY, OR WHAT?

           ___more.   ___same as now.   ___less.   (____)
                                                         48

          I'D LIKE TO ASK THE SAME QUESTIONS IN A SLIGHTLY DIFFER-
          ENT MANNER. IMAGINE A LADDER WITH 10 RUNGS. THE TOP
          RUNG, No. 10, REPRESENTS THE IDEAL LIFE AND THE BOTTOM
          RUNG, No. 1, REPRESENTS THE WORST POSSIBLE LIFE. ON
          WHAT RUNG DO YOU THINK YOU ARE NOW; ON WHAT RUNG WERE
          YOU WHEN YOU LEFT COLLEGE; ON WHAT RUNG WILL YOU BE IN
          5 YEARS?   (____)
                                                                        49

   72-a. #_____ rung now.   (____)
      b. #_____ rung when left the University.   50
      c. #_____ rung 5 years from now.   (____)
                                                               51

THIS BRINGS US NEAR THE END. BEFORE WE STOP, I'D LIKE
TO ASK YOU SOME RATHER GENERAL QUESTIONS.

73.   WHICH OF YOUR ACCOMPLISHMENTS ARE YOU MOST PROUD

      OF? _____   (___)
                                                  52

      _____

Probe, eg, "Which of the areas that we
have discussed--work, education, marriage,
family, recreation, avocation, etc."

74.   WHAT PERSONAL ATTRIBUTES HAVE HELPED YOU THE

      MOST?_____   (__I__)
                                                 53 54

      _____

75.   WHAT PERSONAL ATTRIBUTES HAVE STOOD IN YOUR WAY?
      _____   (__I__)
                                                 55 56

      _____

76.   WHAT ASPECTS OF YOUR LIFE GIVE YOU THE MOST

      DISSATISFACTION?_____   (___)
                                                  57

      _____

      _____

77.   WHAT ASPECTS OF YOUR LIFE GIVE YOU THE GREATEST

      SATISFACTION?_____   (___)
                                                  58

      _____

      _____

78.   IF MONEY, OR FAMILY, OR JOB RESPONSIBILITIES
      COULD BE FORGOTTEN FOR A MOMENT, WHAT KIND OF
      LIFE WOULD YOU LIKE TO BE LIVING 5 YEARS FROM

      NOW?_____   (__I__)
                                                 59 60

      _____

79. THAT IS THE LAST QUESTION. DO YOU HAVE ANY
     FURTHER COMMENTS?

_____   (____)
                                              61
_____

Please thank subject for his considerable
time and trouble.

Time interview ended_____

Total time   _____

Date   _____
                    Mo / Day / Year

Please return interview, Minn.Study
Aptitudes Test, Answer sheet, and
Rating scale by first class mail,
immediately, to:

Dr. David Campbell -- PERSONAL
University of Minnesota
101 Eddy Hall
Minneapolis 14, Minnesota

Thank you for your cooperation.

INDEX